Portable Music
& Its Functions

General Editors
Steve Jones
Joli Jensen
Anahid Kassabian
Will Straw

Vol. 6

PETER LANG
New York • Washington, D.C./Baltimore • Bern
Frankfurt am Main • Berlin • Brussels • Vienna • Oxford

ANDREW WILLIAMS

PORTABLE MUSIC
& ITS FUNCTIONS

PETER LANG
New York • Washington, D.C./Baltimore • Bern
Frankfurt am Main • Berlin • Brussels • Vienna • Oxford

Library of Congress Cataloging-in-Publication Data

Williams, Andrew.
Portable music and its functions / Andrew Williams.
p. cm. —(Music/meanings; v. 6)
Includes bibliographical references (p.) and index.
1. Music—Psychological aspects. 2. Digital music players—Social aspects.
3. Music—Social aspects. I. Title.
ML3830.W545   781.5'3—dc22   2006025281
ISBN-13: 978-0-8204-8125-8
ISBN-10: 0-8204-8125-4
ISSN 1531-6726

Bibliographic information published by **Die Deutsche Bibliothek**.
Die Deutsche Bibliothek lists this publication in the "Deutsche
Nationalbibliografie"; detailed bibliographic data is available
on the Internet at http://dnb.ddb.de/.

Cover design by Lorrin Windahl

© 2007 Peter Lang Publishing, Inc., New York
29 Broadway, 18th floor, New York, NY 10006
www.peterlang.com

All rights reserved.
Reprint or reproduction, even partially, in all forms such as microfilm,
xerography, microfiche, microcard, and offset strictly prohibited.

Contents

• Chapter One: Introduction •	**1**
Portable Music	1
Individual Musical Experience	2
Adapting Bull's Analysis to Focus on Music	3
The Functions of Portable Music	4
Data Collection	6
• Chapter Two: Chosen Sounds and Learning •	**8**
Function One: Chosen Sounds	8
Function Two: Learning	11
• Chapter Three: Aestheticisation, Environmental Control, Boundary Demarcation, and Interpersonal Mediation •	**20**
Function Three: Aestheticisation	20
Function Four: Environmental Control	28
Function Five: Boundary Demarcation	41
Function Six: Interpersonal Mediation	55
• Chapter Four: Company, Aural Mnemonic, Mood Management, Time Management and Activation •	**73**
Function Seven: Company	73
Function Eight: Aural Mnemonic	84
Function Nine: Mood Management	91
Function Ten: Time Management	98
Function Eleven: Activation	103
• Chapter Five: Conclusions •	**108**
Bibliography	115
Index	123

• CHAPTER ONE •

Introduction

Portable Music

Transmitted directly to listeners' ears via headphones, portable music transforms the daily experiences of millions of listeners whenever they choose and wherever they find themselves. Using devices such as iPods, Walkmans or derivatives of these, listeners might focus entirely on their chosen music as they listen. Alternatively, listeners might use music to control the sounds of their surroundings, to ease the negotiation of physical environments they perceive as oppressive, or to control personal interactions. In these situations music provides an insular or solipsistic respite. If listeners observe their surroundings while listening, portable music can give them the impression that they are viewing or acting in a film for which their music is the soundtrack. Listeners might choose rhythmic music for motivation during exercise, or music that will influence their mood. Portable music might substitute for a companion, or simply allow a more enjoyable or productive use of time they would otherwise consider wasted. These experiences, and the related functions that music fulfills for individual listeners, are the subjects of this book.

People engage in many activities while they listen to portable music, and the combined, simultaneous experience of portable music and other activities provide the raw data for this study. Comparison between the literature and listeners' perceptions of their experiences is also fundamental, because a great deal of the literature pertaining to portable music is speculative and unsupported by ethnographic data. By mining both ethnographic and theoretical sources, the pertinence or otherwise of the literature can be established and, more importantly, a complete picture can be constructed of the functions that portable music fulfils for listeners.

The iPod is the most significant recent development in the history of portable music technology. Originally released by Apple Computer in 2001, its earliest precursor, in terms of equipment for the playback of recorded music, is the phonograph, developed by Thomas Edison in 1897. Shortly after he invented the phonograph, Edison proposed a list of eleven applications to which it might be suited. The list included purposes such as assisting dictation; providing audio books for the lady or gentleman whose eyes and hands may be otherwise employed; teaching elocution; and preserving the sayings, the voice, and the last words of a dying family member. It is interesting to note that recording and reproducing music, the area in which the phonograph's greatest business potential was ultimately to lie, was fifth on the list. The Walkman was another significant development in the history of the playback of recorded music, particularly so with respect to the focus of this study. The Walkman's release in 1979 was greeted with massive publicity, similar to that seen more recently with the release of the iPod.

Devices such as the Walkman and the iPod are critical to the experience of portable music. They allow mobile listeners to carry their music with them and hear it as they wish. This convenience enables mobile listeners to use portable music in many ways as they feel the need, and the ways in which listeners use portable music, and the functions portable music fulfils for them, are discussed at length below.

Individual Musical Experience

Study of the experience of portable music is generally neglected in the discourse; however, related issues such as the experience of listening to music in general, the experience of listening to recorded music, and the experience of listening to music while engaged in other activities are discussed. Tia DeNora is explicit in her observation of the great potential in the study of solitary listening. She writes:

> Focus on intimate musical practice, on the private or one-to-one forms of human-music interaction, offers an ideal vantage point for viewing music "in action"... (2000:46)

Listening to music using a Walkman or iPod is one example of the private listening or one-to-one human-music interaction that DeNora discusses, and she suggests that such study offers great potential for understanding how listeners construe their musical experiences and the purposes for which they use music. Note that DeNora refers to music in action, thus suggesting that music achieves some purpose for listeners. This study, with its focus on portable music's functions, is another manifestation of this understanding.

Another recommendation to study the experience of listening to recorded music is found in the work of Pekka Gronow. In his study of the recording industry, Gronow makes some observations that have substantial implications for music scholarship. He observes the ubiquity of recorded music and, in doing so, alludes to the potential futility of music scholarship that ignores it. Gronow writes that 'Records and music are becoming almost synonymous' (1983:72) and 'Today it is impossible to think of almost any type of music without considering the role of recordings' (1983:72). For these reasons, the study of listening to recorded music assumes an importance that has previously been unacknowledged. This is a study of a particular type of recorded music. Portable music is always recorded music, always chosen by the mobile listener, and always heard using headphones or earphones and a device such as an iPod or Walkman.

Adapting Bull's Analysis to Focus on Music

Michael Bull has written prolifically regarding various aspects of the Walkman, and he produces several analyses that classify the strategies of Walkman use. Observing that a Walkman user may listen for different reasons at different times or for more than one reason at once, Bull acknowledges that the strategies he proposes '... can slide imperceptibly into another' (2000:186). Using his system of analysis, Bull is nonetheless able to identify eleven strategies of Walkman listening. However, as suggested by his focus on Walkman listening, Bull concentrates exclusively on the Walkman, to the neglect of the music that Walkman users choose to hear. Bull's system of classification is useful if it is adapted to acknowledge music's role in listeners' experiences, and it is modified here to analyse the functions of portable music.

This study's definition of portable music is premised on the inseparable combination of music (content) and the means of its reproduction (medium), and Rebecca Lind's ideas on the role of music for Walkman users are relevant here. At one point Lind takes a similar position to that taken in this study, observing that '... content and medium may be considered as inseparable' (1989:38). This understanding of the importance of the roles of portable music and the device that transmits it is inverted relative to the ideas of many writers such as Bull, who write excitedly about the latest technological developments. A Walkman or iPod amounts to very little beyond a lump of plastic and other materials without music or other content for it to reproduce. Moreover, many of the functions that Bull and Lind ascribe to the Walkman have analogies that are carried out by music when it is transmitted by other means. Recognising the importance of music's role for the many listeners who choose iPods or Walkmans to hear it, this study now turns to an analysis of portable music's functions.

The Functions of Portable Music

Listeners focus on their portable music in the first two of portable music's functions. In **chosen sounds**, portable music is simply the mobile listener's chosen listening material and, as such, fulfillment of the mobile listener's desire to hear it. A listener wants to hear particular recorded music and uses the Walkman or iPod in order to do so. The second function, **learning**, stands alone in this study in that its definition is not derived from Bull's (2000) typology of the strategies of Walkman use. The need for an additional function became apparent when this study's interview results were analysed, since a significant number could not be classified according to the functions Bull defined. In learning, portable music functions as the subject of the listener's attempts to learn it. Typically, although not necessarily, a music student, the mobile listener listens to portable music in an attempt to become familiar with it and to understand it. The listener can learn the structure and form of the work, attempt to make aural sense of theoretical information regarding the music, compare interpretations or stylistic variations, and generally familiarise her/himself with it.

The next four functions of portable music involve listeners' interactions with their environments and surroundings. **Aestheticisation** is the listener's construction of a unique perception of their environment, combining their surroundings with portable music. There are two aspects of aestheticisation to consider. In the first, portable music combines with the visual environment within which listening occurs. In effects they frequently liken to watching or being in a film or film clip, listeners hear portable music while observing their surroundings. In the second, portable music combines with the aural elements of the listener's environment that are not filtered out by their headphones or earphones. In this way the listener notices an auricular combination of portable music and ambient noise.

In **environmental control**, listeners choose to replace external ambient sounds with portable music so the music acts as an alternative soundscape, preferred by listeners to environmental sounds they consider unpleasant.

In **boundary demarcation**, listeners feel that portable music can set them apart from their surroundings. Portable music demarcates no literal or physical boundary around them, but listeners feel removed from unpleasant environments nonetheless. Public transport frequently recurs in mobile listeners' accounts of their listening as the setting for boundary demarcation.

In the sixth function, **interpersonal mediation**, portable music mediates personal interaction in two ways. First, because listeners' attention is directed toward their music and not toward their environments, they are more difficult to approach. This may be unintentional, with mobile listeners unaware of the reduced attention they pay to bystanders. Conversely, this may be intentional, with mobile listeners deliberately choosing to listen to portable music with the express purpose of eliminating undesirable personal interaction. Second, portable music may render the listener unable to hear others' verbal attempts to gain their attention by overwhelming external noises. Although listeners may otherwise choose to interact, they remain unaware of the opportunity to do so. The Walkman or iPod apparatus also plays a role in interpersonal mediation. Its presence, visible to bystanders, indicates the mobile listener's intention to listen to portable music as well as the consequent reduced attention they pay to their surroundings. For bystanders, the listener's portable music plays no role in any subsequent modification of social interaction because, apart from leakage, they cannot hear it. Nonetheless, bystanders interpret the presence of iPod or Walkman paraphernalia to mean mobile listeners are focused on something other than the potential for social interaction. Bystanders modify or reduce their attempts to interact with the listener accordingly, considering any such attempts unnecessarily difficult and potentially wasted.

Mobile listeners focus on themselves in the final five functions of portable music. **Company** is mobile listeners' perception of the presence of the musicians whose music they listen to. Listeners use portable music as a substitute companion. This perception occurs despite the temporal and spatial separation between listeners and the musicians who recorded the portable music in question.

In **aural mnemonic**, certain music becomes associated in listeners' minds with events from their pasts. When heard subsequently from a Walkman or iPod, the music reminds them of those events. Portable music triggers feelings and emotions as well as memories.

In **mood management**, mobile listeners use portable music to modify undesirable moods or to sustain moods they enjoy.

In **time management**, mobile listeners choose to listen to portable music instead of resigning themselves to complete lack of activity or instead of undertaking activities they consider boring or monotonous. Listeners consider their portable music to be a relatively more productive occupation than other alternatives.

Finally, in **activation**, portable music, especially when it is rhythmic in nature, stimulates movement in mobile listeners. They move to the rhythm of the music and may undertake more strenuous physical activity as a result.

Data Collection

Interviews were carried out to ensure that the individual experience of portable music's functions would be comprehensively examined and accurately described. The interviews enabled the functions of portable music, derived as most of them are from the literature, to be tested against the perceptions of real-world mobile listeners. The only criteria applied to the selection of interview subjects were that they used a Walkman, iPod or derivative device to listen to music and were willing to participate. Twenty-six listeners were interviewed between May and November 2001. Fifteen were students of The University of Adelaide in Australia and one other a staff member of the same university. Four subjects worked together in a design office and two others were family members of one of these designers. The remainder were acquaintances of other interviewees. Of the twenty-six respondents, sixteen were male. Interviews were carried out face-to-face, by telephone or e-mail correspondence. The interviews were informally structured but each was directed toward ascertaining the mobile listener's own understanding of their reasons for using portable music and therefore the functions that portable music fulfils for them. Qualitative analysis of the interview data was deemed the most effective way to extract relevant and useful information that could subsequently be compared against the literature. Respondents constructed their understanding of their listening experiences to the interviewer, who provided only limited prompting to ensure the discussion remained relevant to the study.

· CHAPTER TWO ·

Chosen Sounds and Learning

Two functions of portable music—chosen sounds and learning—are examined in this chapter. These are the only functions in which portable music is the focus of mobile listeners' attention. In chosen sounds, listeners concentrate on their portable music because they enjoy listening to it. In learning, listeners concentrate on their portable music because they are studying it. Initially it may seem anomalous that portable music has only two functions in which it is the mobile listener's sole focus. However, as demonstrated in subsequent chapters, portable music's functionality for listeners extends far beyond providing listening material.

Function One: Chosen Sounds

The most straightforward of portable music's functions is chosen sounds. In this function, portable music is simply something mobile listeners enjoy. They want to hear it and use their Walkmans or iPods to do so; portable music is the fulfillment of listeners' desires to hear it. Note that chosen sounds is the function of portable music that most often occurs in combination with other functions. Intuitively, it is clear that mobile listeners will listen to their choice of music. Therefore, portable music will always function as chosen sounds, even as it functions simultaneously in other ways. This concurrence of multiple functions exemplifies Bull's observation regarding the nature of classificatory analysis as discussed in Chapter One; that is, '... one example can slide imperceptibly into another' (2000:186). The only distinction between chosen sounds and listeners' enjoyment of music in any other situation is that the chosen music is portable music and thus facilitates listeners' desires to hear it in virtually any situation. Further, because portable music is always the listener's chosen music, it simultaneously functions as listeners' chosen sounds even as it

•CHAPTER TWO•

fulfils other functions. In this manner, chosen sounds describes at least a part of all mobile listening.

The perception of music as a source of enjoyment is so fundamental that it is rarely documented. Apart from a few interview responses, this investigation found only four sources in which this premise was explicitly discussed, although it was often implicit. These four sources reflect the contemporary social perception of music as the source of enjoyable experience as well as the historical basis of that perception. First, Aristotle briefly observes 'Most men nowadays take part in music for the sake of the pleasure it gives ...' (1992 [c330BC]:455). This is an early observation of the pleasure that listeners take in music, and their resulting desire to play or hear it. Aristotle's words could apply in a discussion of contemporary listeners and there is no doubt that enjoyment still motivates many listeners' efforts to hear music.

Second, in an earlier edition of *The New Grove Dictionary of Music and Musicians*, Sparshott reviews the field of musical aesthetics. He understands that the fundamental question for the field '... must be the nature of the musical work itself' (1980:120) and subsequently suggests several possibilities for that nature. One possibility is that the musical work is '... essentially an object of a certain sort, an achieved reality which, once made, may be understood and enjoyed for whatever it is ...' (1980:120–121). Here Sparshott expresses the basis of chosen sounds; for many listeners, portable music is something they enjoy hearing and this enjoyment motivates their listening. Next, in a survey of philosophies of music in the subsequent edition of *The New Grove Dictionary of Music and Musicians*, Stephen Davies writes that '... musical works are valued for the pleasure that attends their appreciation' (2001a:623). Davies does not comment on the musical work itself, but on the manner in which listeners receive it. He observes that listeners value, appreciate, and enjoy listening to music, corresponding to the manner in which mobile listeners experience their portable music in chosen sounds. Finally Alan Merriam, as noted in the introduction, discusses ten functions of music from an ethnomusicological perspective. Of particular interest here is what Merriam names 'The function of entertainment' (1964:223). He writes 'Music provides an entertainment function in all societies' (1964:223) and chosen sounds is one example of this. Mobile listeners use portable music because it entertains them or occupies them in an agreeable manner. Chosen sounds, then, is a relatively recent and technologically advanced manifestation of a function which music has held at least since the days of Aristotle and, following Merriam, which it continues to hold in every society. The four sources reviewed above represent a meagre return regarding the view that music is a source of enjoyment for listeners. As noted however, the scarcity of relevant sources can be read as an indication that the view of music as a source of enjoyment is so fundamental as to be infrequently documented.

In addition to individual listeners' accounts, cited below, aspects of Lind's and Bull's examinations of the Walkman are pertinent to chosen sounds. In her study, Lind posed the research question: 'What are the functions of the personal stereo for college students who use such devices?' (1989:55). She conducted telephone interviews and surveyed the frequency with which her respondents' reasons for using their Walkmans corresponded to fourteen reasons she formulated in advance. As noted previously, some of Lind's proposed reasons for Walkman use relate to the functions of portable music examined here and further instances of similarity are noted as other functions are examined. Relative to chosen sounds, Lind found that two common reasons for Walkman use are that 'you can listen to what you want, when you want to' (1989:59) and 'it [the Walkman] allows you to listen to music while you're "on the go"' (1989:59). Both reasons correspond to chosen sounds. Bull makes similar observations:

> Users describe being absorbed in the pleasure of listening uninterruptedly to their own auditized flow of experience. These users prefer to hear their "own" music whilst on the move. They may or may not take notice of their environment but more often than not they merely attend to their music. Personal-stereo use satisfies user's desires for their chosen sound accompaniment wherever they might be. (2000:187)

Enjoyment of portable music motivates such listeners to use the Walkman. Despite their focus on the Walkman apparatus rather than on the music it transmits, in the discussions cited above both Bull and Lind are forced to acknowledge portable music because it is important for the listeners to whom they refer.

As noted, portable music functions as chosen sounds when mobile listeners are motivated by simple enjoyment of portable music. Three mobile listeners professed this motivation in interviews for this study. For example, Daniel stated:

> For me, the Walkman is just the logical outcome of how I feel about music. I mean, I'm studying it here at the Con[1], I play in bands and go out to hear bands. I just love music and with the Walkman I can listen to more of it. (2001)

Daniel's love of music is his main motivation for listening to portable music at times when he cannot participate in music in other ways. He desires constant exposure to music and portable music suits him because it can be heard in almost every situation. Jessica explained her motivation for mobile listening in similar terms:

> Well, I love music. I know that sounds really dumb but it's one of my passions. It's about the music. (2001)

Daniel's and Jessica's mobile listening are excellent examples, and clearly demonstrate the principles of chosen sounds.

Erin's account of her Walkman listening is the final example of mobile listening for the sake of the music alone, and thus of chosen sounds. Erin listens to portable music on public transport. Asked whether she prefers to commute with or without portable music, Erin responds:

> I prefer to have it with me actually. I like listening to music on the bus. I like listening to music anyway and so if I listen to music on the bus I get to listen to more music. (2001)

Many mobile listeners use portable music on public transport to block out surroundings they consider unpleasant (this phenomenon is examined in Chapter Three in the discussion of boundary demarcation). Other mobile listeners choose to listen on public transport because they feel their listening is more productive use of time they would otherwise consider wasted (this phenomenon is examined in Chapter Four in the discussion of time management). By contrast, Erin's only motivation for listening is her enjoyment of her portable music and Erin's portable music thus functions only as her chosen sounds.

Function Two: Learning

In this function portable music is the focus of the listener's attempts to learn it. Listeners are typically music students who listen to portable music in order to make aural sense of theoretical information about it. In many cases the resulting knowledge is applied toward the listener's studies and subsequent performance of the music. When the interviews were analysed it became apparent that a significant cohort of the mobile listeners interviewed (10 out of 26) listened to their portable music to learn it. Note that fourteen respondents of the total of twenty-six were music students. This weighting of the sample group explains learning's inclusion here and its exclusion from other related studies such as Bull's and Lind's, in which it is possible, even likely, that no music students were included. For instance, Aliese, a typical example of this cohort of music student respondents, was attempting to familiarise herself with the string quartet repertoire for her PhD studies. She stated:

> At the moment I'm going to really have to start listening to these tapes of the string quartets because I want to know the repertoire. The reason I taped it is because I know I'm more likely to listen to it on my Walkman than if I have to keep going down to the library. (2001)

Aliese carries her Walkman around with her. This means she can listen to the music she wants to study whenever she gets an idle moment rather than having to make a special effort. Portable music's convenience allows Aliese to listen more than would otherwise be possible and thus optimise her study efforts.

In her interview, Glenyce drew a comparison between listening on a home stereo system and on a Walkman:

> It's much more direct on a Walkman. The more direct approach, well, I think it's better for learning actually. It makes you focus a lot better. I tend to get distracted quite easily so it's a good learning tool for me. (2001)

When she tries to learn music, Glenyce appreciates the Walkman's direct transmission of music to her ears. The Walkman's headphones shut out ambient noise and thus remove possible distractions. Glenyce feels she concentrates more effectively on her portable music than she would on recorded music not transmitted by headphones and learns it more thoroughly as a result.

Finally, Scott illustrated an important facet of learning. He related:

> [When I'm listening] I might be thinking about how I'd play it [the portable music]. Because I'm a musician I'm thinking of what I'd be doing in that situation. I think of transcribing what I'm hearing or playing it myself. (2001)

• CHAPTER TWO • 13

As he listens, Scott attempts to learn his portable music from the perspective of a performer. Whereas Aliese attempts to become familiar with certain music and understand it in theoretical terms, Scott aims to develop his own playing by first understanding, then imitating and possibly improving on what he hears.

In contrast to these positive listener comments, several significant composers expressed negative opinions regarding recorded music's impact on music education and training in response to the gramophone's initial development. The thrust of the criticism was that the gramophone would eliminate traditional music teaching and the experiences of hearing live music and of playing music with others. John Philip Sousa is particularly vehement, writing:

> I foresee a marked deterioration in American music and musical taste, an interruption in the musical development of the country, and a host of other injuries to music in its artistic manifestations, by virtue—or rather by vice—of the multiplication of the various music reproducing machines. (1906:278)

Sousa predicts this deterioration will occur because listening to recorded music will substitute for the study of the practice of music:

> The child becomes indifferent to practice, for when music can be heard in the homes without the labor of study and close application, and without the slow process of acquiring a technic, it will be simply a question of time when the amateur disappears entirely, and with him a host of vocal and instrumental teachers, who will be without field or calling. (1906:280)

Sousa feels a music student's efforts to master an instrument are motivated by the desire to hear music; however, it seems more likely that music students are motivated by the desire to master an instrument and play music. Thus, the opportunity the gramophone provides to hear more music than was previously possible might not have been as disastrous for amateur musicianship as Sousa predicted. In fact, the ability to hear otherwise unavailable music cannot be considered anything other than a boon for musicianship of any level. Nonetheless, Sousa's concerns are shared by others. Béla Bartók is also wary of the gramophone's effects on performance. In an essay on "Mechanical Music" he writes:

> The propagation of the radio and gramophone would have a very great drawback if it caused people to give up performing instead of arousing a longing to play music. (1976:296)

Unlike Sousa, Bartók sees potential for recorded music to have a positive as well as a negative influence on musical participation; recordings might arouse the desire to play music. Although critical of recordings as they compare with live music, Bartók sees a role for them in teaching and learning music. He writes:

> Although the very best gramophone records can never replace the original performance from an aesthetic point of view, they still must be considered as a surrogate. The role of the gramophone is more important from the pedagogic and scientific point of view. (1976:292)

Bartók employs the by now familiar device of comparing recorded music to live music. In this comparison he notes deficiencies in recorded music on the grounds of aesthetics but, foreshadowing learning and the listening practices of many music students in particular, he notes its usefulness to pedagogy. Apart from anything else, recorded music enables music students to hear the music they are studying while they study it. This measure of convenience was impossible before recording and, as noted, portable music facilitates even more convenient listening. As Aliese attested, using the Walkman or iPod, students can take advantage of convenient listening and study whenever and wherever the motivation strikes.

Igor Stravinsky also criticises recorded music—not from an aesthetic point of view in the manner of Bartók, but rather in response to his observations of changes in the process of hearing music. Stravinsky observes a downside to the easy availability of recorded music, and writes:

> In John [sic] Sebastian Bach's day it was necessary for him to walk ten miles to a neighboring town to hear Buxtehude play his works. Today anyone, living no matter where, has only to turn a knob or put on a record to hear what he likes. Indeed, it is in just this incredible facility, this lack of necessity for any effort, that the evil of this so-called progress lies. For in music, more than in any other branch of art, understanding is given only to those who make an active effort. Passive receptivity is not enough. To listen to certain combinations of sound and automatically become accustomed to them does not necessarily imply that they have been heard and understood. (1962:152–153)

Stravinsky seems to feel that the effort required by Bach to walk to the next town contributed to his understanding of Buxtehude's works. By contrast, it is likely the exertion involved in walking ten miles to a church service or concert could, in fact, promote passive listening, induced by fatigue, of the kind Stravinsky clearly deplores. It is also possible that many mobile listeners, listening to their portable music in the circumstances most convenient to them, could listen actively with a great deal of critical awareness and insight. Stravinsky's criticisms of recorded music and its consequences for music education seem reactionary in light of the contemporary assimilation of recorded music into everyday life and music scholarship.

In some ways, Ralph Vaughan Williams' understanding of the pitfalls of attempting to learn music by listening to recordings are similar to those of Stravinsky, although his opinion differs in one important facet. He writes:

> In those days, before the gramophone and the wireless and the miniature score, the pianoforte duet was the only way, unless you were an orchestral player, of getting to know orchestral music, and one really got to know it from the inside, not in the superficial way of lazily listening to a gramophone record. (1963:183)

As noted, Stravinsky is critical of learning music through listening to recordings in comparison to hearing live music. With a slightly different emphasis, Vaughan Williams criticises recorded music as a learning tool in comparison with active participation in music making. Vaughan Williams feels that actually playing the music with another pianist in the form of piano duet reductions of orchestral scores is the best way to gain an understanding of the music. Compared with this method, he considers listening to recorded music on a gramophone to be irredeemably lazy. Of the composers whose views are reviewed above, Vaughan Williams' are the most sensible. Convenient listening, in the manner enabled by the Walkman or iPod and the gramophone before them, does not necessarily detract from the learning of music. It is accepted here, however, that listening alone does not comprise a complete musical education and should be accompanied by other practical and theoretical studies. Nonetheless, the convenience with which students can hear recordings of the music they are studying can only assist their learning efforts.

In his essay, "The Curves of the Needle", Adorno also makes observations pertaining to the use of recorded music as a means of learning. He observes a change in musical participation due to the gramophone's increasing ubiquity and suggests the gramophone is:

> ... a utensil of the private life that regulates the consumption of art in the nineteenth century. It is the bourgeois family that gathers around the

gramophone in order to enjoy the music that it itself—as was already the case in the feudal household—is unable to perform. (1990a:50)

Adorno's observation is still pertinent despite his reference to the listening practices of the nineteenth century and his use of anachronistic class distinctions. Many people who use Walkmans, iPods or other means of reproducing recorded music are unable to play the music they hear. Unlike the composers reviewed above, Adorno does not attribute the musical incompetence of this bourgeois family to the advent of the gramophone, observing that, in feudal times before the development of any means of music recording, people were also unable to play music which they might have heard played by professional musicians. Adorno thus demonstrates why recorded music should not be considered the downfall of music education in the way Sousa and others thought when it was first developed and introduced.

Adorno also makes observations relevant to learning in "Opera and the Long Playing Record". He observes that the introduction of the long-playing record meant:

> The entire musical literature could now become available in quite-authentic form to listeners desirous of auditioning and studying such works at a time convenient to them. (1990c:63)

Here Adorno makes several relevant points. First, Adorno's reference to the use of recordings to study musical works is a direct acknowledgment of recorded music's role in music education. Learning, using portable music, is one particular example of this general capacity of recorded music. Second, Adorno's observation of the long-playing record's 'quite-authentic form' acknowledges that musical works, previously artificially shortened and broken up in order to fit on record sides of restricted capacity, are now recorded complete and uninterrupted. Subsequent technological developments such as the CD, minidisc, and mp3 have removed capacity limitations even further into the memories of early listeners. 'Quite-authentic', though, is a somewhat reserved and two-edged approbation. Along with Adorno's observation that recordings enable listeners to 'audition' works, it implies a belief that live performance maintains some kind of superiority over recordings. Adorno suggests recordings can aid listeners in decisions whether or not to hear a live performance of the work in question. Recordings can also familiarise listeners with the work that they will subsequently hear in live performance. Recordings are thus an appetiser for the 'real thing' but not a meal in themselves, despite their usefulness to students of music. Finally, recordings allow people to listen to music at times convenient to them. Continuing the theme of convenience, recordings are particularly useful in the study of music because:

> The ability to repeat long-playing records, as well as parts of them, fosters a familiarity which is hardly afforded by the ritual of performance. (1990c:64)

Once again, recorded music serves music education well because of its convenience. Students can hear the music they are studying in the classroom as their teacher discusses it. Students need not wait for a local or touring ensemble to play particular music but can hear it at their leisure and repeat it many times if they desire.

Further insight into the individual experience of learning can be gained from the accounts of mobile listening from this study's interviews. Aliese, whose efforts to familiarise herself with the string quartet repertoire are noted above, thought that using her Walkman to learn music was more effective than other listening techniques. She related:

> At first the whole string quartet repertoire was incomprehensible. You can't tell one person from the other—Beethoven, whatever. But I know that if I listen to it enough I can get the hang of it and I know that the only medium I'm going to listen to it on is my Walkman. Even when I'm sitting there in the library doing nothing, reading the liner notes, whatever, I'm not thinking about the music. But if I'm on the train or whatever I'm just sort of staring into space but really, really concentrating on each note and how they're all working against each other. (2001)

Aliese finds her most concentrated learning efforts take place in situations where she is least likely to be distracted. She has taken her train journey so many times she is thoroughly familiar with the route and can direct her attention completely toward her portable music. For Aliese, portable music's convenience and portability optimises her learning because it allows her to study in the environments she considers most conducive.

Miriam also discussed her Walkman use:

> If I need to learn a piece for uni or something I'll pop it on and listen to it over and over again until I get it into my head. That way I can actually hear it and save time because I'm travelling and doing work while I'm travelling. (2001)

Miriam considers that her mobile listening, especially because it is directly related to her studies, is a more constructive use of time which would otherwise be devoted only to commuting. The capacity that portable music gives listeners to make productive use of time they would otherwise consider wasted is termed time management and discussed extensively in Chapter Four. Note that Miriam explicitly thinks of listening to music as working. Miriam's portable music is her course material, equivalent to a textbook, and her listening is study.

Aaron's interview introduces an idea that stretches the concept of the use of portable stereo devices in learning. Like Scott, noted above, he related his listening back to himself and his own musical efforts, although to a much greater extent. Discussing his Walkman use, which directly relates to his violin studies, Aaron told:

> I've got an MD [minidisc] Walkman which I primarily use to record my own performances or other performances as well as copying recordings that I get a hold of from the library. I tend to use that on a daily basis, taking it everywhere as a form of documentation. I especially use it in performance to get another perspective of my own playing. This can be really helpful. (2001)

Aaron explains how recording and subsequently listening to and reviewing his own performances is helpful to him:

> You're your own best critic. You always hear your mistakes very clearly. The littlest thing you don't like is immediately apparent, which to me is perfect. Being able to hear them and think about it—"Why did I do that? How did it happen?"—only goes to further my own playing and performing abilities. (2001)

To this point this study has discussed only portable music heard by listeners once other musicians have recorded it and the technological advance represented by portable listening devices has been discussed only in terms of the mobile listening it affords. Now Aaron's listening demonstrates another level of the application of this technology. In addition to its mobility, Aaron exploits his Walkman's recording capabilities in order to review his own performances. Thus, he learns about himself and his performance techniques and subsequently improves as a musician. This, while it differs slightly from other mobile listening documented in this study, is still learning and, in addition to every other example of the use of portable music examined here, demonstrates the application of available technologies by individual users to their own ends.

Notes

[1] 'The Con' is the Elder School of Music, formerly The Elder Conservatorium at The University of Adelaide.

• CHAPTER THREE •

Aestheticisation, Environmental Control, Boundary Demarcation, and Interpersonal Mediation

The four functions of portable music examined in Chapter Three exemplify the ways mobile listeners modify their interactions with various aspects of their environments. In aestheticisation, listeners construct a unique perception of their surroundings by combining them with portable music. In environmental control, listeners choose to replace external ambient sounds with portable music. In boundary demarcation, listeners use portable music to set them apart from their surroundings, especially when they consider those surroundings to be unpleasant. Finally, in interpersonal mediation, listeners use portable music to modify their personal interactions with people in their vicinity. Having examined in Chapter Two those functions of portable music in which mobile listeners' aim is to listen to their music, in this chapter mobile listeners' engagement in social interactions where solitude and solipsism might have been expected is frequently observed.

Function Three: Aestheticisation

In aestheticisation, portable music functions in two closely related modes. In the first, mobile listeners observe their surroundings while listening to portable music and thus experience something similar to watching a film or video. Portable music is thus the aural component or 'soundtrack' of this filmic experience, and listeners' surroundings the visual component. In aestheticisation's second mode, portable music combines with those aural elements of listeners' surroundings that are still audible over their portable music. Listeners thus hear an aural 'collage', comprising a combination of portable music and ambient environmental noise. In both modes, aestheticisation is the listener's experience of their environment as it combines with the sounds of their portable music.

Describing his mode of Walkman use that is adapted here as aestheticisation, Bull writes:

> Users sometimes describe their experience as particularly pleasurable ... as an aesthetic experience. Users often pick music to "suit" the environment passed through. (2000:188)

He also writes 'Personal stereos used in this way permits [sic] the promotion of aesthetic or "filmic" experience' (2000:188). Three important points arise from Bull's observations. First, and as noted previously, even though Bull presents strategies of 'personal-stereo use' (2000:186), he mentions music when describing this strategy: 'Users often pick music to "suit" the environment passed through' (2000:188). Portable music, not just the Walkman apparatus, is the key to aestheticisation and Bull's discussion implicitly acknowledges this. Second, Bull describes this strategy in terms of '... an aesthetic experience' (2000:188). It is noteworthy that listeners consider their surroundings to be of aesthetic significance when combined with their portable music. This is an indication of music's capacity to transform listeners' everyday experiences from mundane to vivid and captivating. Finally, Bull describes this form of mobile musical experience as 'filmic'. This description recurs frequently in discussions related to aestheticisation's first mode. For example, Moebius and Michel-Annen also draw the comparison between the experience of listening to portable music and watching a film, writing:

> Life is changed into a cinema event. Contact with reality decreases, Walkman users feel that they are the audience at a movie as voyeurs. (1994:572)

Other examples of this comparison are reviewed at various stages throughout the discussion of aestheticisation's first mode.

Also relevant, Chen presents the example of Terry, a subject of her study, who recounts:

> Sitting outside my apartment watching things happen. I have my headsets on so as not to hear anything but to just see what is happening. With not hearing anything but the music you can try to match the song to something that is going on around me at that moment. (1993:105)

This is a clear example of the first mode of aestheticisation. Terry's portable music, in combination with the surroundings in which he hears it, creates a unique and aesthetic aural and visual experience. It also supports Bull's observation that listeners choose music to suit their surroundings.

Listening practices similar to aestheticisation, but involving live music or forms of recorded music existing prior to the development of the Walkman or iPod, can be considered aestheticisation's precursors. The first such example is related by Eisenberg, who observes:

> When a record is fitted over the platter, a transparency or slide is fitted over a segment of space and time. The effect is a double exposure. But if the music is worth its salt, it will assert itself as the true reality, and all the lovely furniture of one's room will seem (if one is aware of it at all) a mere picture ... (1988:251)

Eisenberg discusses fitting a record over a platter. This is a reference to playing an LP on a turntable, but Eisenberg's insights are pertinent to music in any form, live or recorded. Recorded music simply allows listeners to achieve the transformation Eisenberg discusses at their convenience, while live music demands that listeners wait until musicians play it. Importantly, note Eisenberg understands that listeners perceive music, rather than their mundane surroundings, as 'reality'. This is a triumph for music rather than its unfortunate dismissal to the background. Eisenberg's reference to the listener's surroundings as a 'picture', with its connotations of artistic beauty, emphasises the aesthetic nature of this experience of recorded music. Also note Eisenberg employs an analogy of photography in his reference to 'a double exposure'. This relates closely to the 'film' analogy that best and frequently explains aestheticisation's first mode.

In the context of a discussion regarding the continuing vitality of twelve-tone, serial and expressionist music, Barbiero observes a shift in music's role in listeners' daily lives. He writes:

> Music has become a background texture for daily life, and we tend to hear it as we hear a film soundtrack: as a supplement to action within the frame. (1989:147)

Barbiero does not support his assertion with empirical evidence, but intuition suggests it is not unreasonable. In fact, Adorno made the same observation several years earlier in "On the Fetish-Character in Music and the Regression of Listening", writing music '... is perceived

•CHAPTER THREE• 23

purely as background' (1978:271). Despite its affinity with Adorno, Barbiero's position should not be taken as the only perspective on this question. It is noted above that Eisenberg, for one, has a different opinion. He suggests that listeners' surroundings fade into the background while their music asserts '... itself as the true reality ...' (1988:251). It seems probable that different listeners have different focuses, which may also vary with different listening circumstances. Despite these varying possibilities, Barbiero's use of the word 'supplement', as cited above, to describe music's role for listeners clearly expresses its function in aestheticisation. Music supplements listeners' interactions with their environments, creating unique aesthetic experiences.

In the final pre-Walkman and iPod source examined in relation to aestheticisation's first mode, Jan Morris describes her own experience of listening to recorded music:

> ... when I drove for the first time down the coast of Yugoslavia, from Istria to Montenegro, I had just acquired a recording, by Vladimir Ashkenazy with the Philharmonia Orchestra, of one of Mozart's piano concertos, I forget which. The allegro movement of this piece contained a tremendously vivacious solo run, cascading from one end of the piano to the other, which was repeated several times and which absolutely suited, it seemed to me, the swashbuckling landscape of karst, sea and island through which my white BMW was sweeping. (1989:33)

Morris' account relates closely to Bull's strategy of Walkman use which is adapted here to define aestheticisation. Bull observes that listeners '... often pick music to "suit" the environment passed through' (2000:188). Morris' description of her driving experience is a vivid account of how listeners might feel that their music suits their environment in the manner Bull discusses. It is also an excellent account of the experience of music in combination with the visual elements of the surroundings.

Aestheticisation can sometimes involve a certain quality of social interaction for mobile listeners. A writer for *The New Yorker* relates an account of her mobile listening that demonstrates this phenomenon. She first presents her experience in terms that explicitly suggest aestheticisation's first mode, writing '... when I listen to the Walkman I'm not just tuning out. I'm also tuning in a soundtrack for the scenery around me' (Anon. 1989:20). The writer compares her portable music to the music of a stage production and understands it as remarkably appropriate musical and lyrical accompaniment for what she sees around her. Two social aspects of mobile listening, generally considered a solitary experience, are captured in this writer's account of a particular listening incident:

> I was walking down Sixth Avenue and "High Hopes" was on [my Walkman]—a song I had thought was a little foolish, to tell the truth—and right in front of me were two men struggling to carry two six-foot-high rubber-tree plants. The plants swayed, and then the men swayed from side to side as they tried to balance them, and just then I heard "Whoops, there goes another rubber-tree plant". I only wish every single person passing them on the street could have heard that song. (Anon. 1989:20)

The writer is the only one who can completely hear her portable music. This is an undeniably private aspect of her listening experience. However, the unwitting involvement of the two tree-carrying workers in her listening experience lends it a social aspect. In this instance the social relations are not mutual because the workers are not aware of their involvement. The writer's particular experience of portable music depends on the participation, though unintentional, of others and is thus a social experience. Another instance of a social aspect to this particular experience of mobile listening is manifest in the writer's wish that '... every single person passing them [the rubber tree carrying workers] on the street could have heard that song' (1989). This element of the listening experience is not aestheticisation because the listener does not specifically relate her portable music to her environment in the manner of a film. Nonetheless, her portable music makes such an impression that it causes her to wish people in her vicinity could experience it. Again, this is not typical social interaction because it is not mutual. It is, however, an instance where listening to portable music is not solitary or solipsistic but confirms the listener's existence with other people within a shared environment.

Giles Smith provides an autobiographical account of mobile listening that corresponds to aestheticisation's first mode. Discussing a time when he was sick, he writes:

> A friend bought me a Walkman to cheer me up, the first one I ever had. It struck me, even before I owned one, that the Walkman was, after the in-car stereo, probably the finest technical achievement of the twentieth century—about as refined as man was ever going to get. Without having to go in for bells on our fingers and bells on our toes (cumbersome and, let's face it, not all that satisfying, musically speaking), we could have music wherever we went. On my way to and from the endless clinics and surgeries, I played

almost to ribbons an old cassette of Deniece Williams's ineffably joyful "Let's Hear It For The Boy" (the way the words snap against the beat!) and sat there, clamped between the skinny plastic headphones, enjoying its friendly, life-affirming fizz. I could stare out of the windows of the bus and the world would turn into a video, which is not the kind of perspective you would want all the time, maybe, but which seemed wondrously absorbing at this point. (1995:152)

Note Smith's reference to his listening experience as a video. As a rule, the writers reviewed in this study do not delve more deeply into their listening experiences than to draw this analogy. Nonetheless, it clearly identifies the writers' listening experiences as instances of aestheticisation's first mode.

This study's interviews generated accounts of listening practice that exemplified aestheticisation's first mode. Aliese recounted:

I sort of think that people fit into what I listen to. I thought that the other day when I was watching this lady walk. I was listening to Groove Armada and she wasn't stepping in time with it but the music really fit what she was doing. It was just this lady walking along and I automatically thought that it would make a really good video-clip. (2001)

Note that Aliese used the analogy of a video-clip to describe her experience. In her interview, Bettina also drew an analogy between her mobile listening and a video-clip. However, in the matter of her perspective, Bettina's account of her listening differed from that of Aliese and others reviewed here. Rather than the perspective of a viewer of a video-clip, Bettina had the impression of active involvement *in* the clip. She commented:

... sometimes it [listening to portable music] used to make me feel like I was in a music video-clip, as an active member. (2001)

It is interesting to speculate regarding how mobile listeners would describe their experiences had the analogies of films or video-clips not been available, and musical theatre might provide the answer. In the manner of the *New Yorker* writer reviewed above, the interviewees and writers reviewed here might understand their experiences in terms of viewing a particularly life-like musical theatre production, while Bettina might picture herself performing in one.

As noted, Bull's strategies of Walkman use are the basis of most of the functions of portable music examined in this study and aestheticisation's first mode is one such function. Bull's writing, however, suggests nothing of aestheticisation's second mode. Consideration of this mode was prompted by the writing of Steve Connor and this study's interview results, where listeners recounted experiencing portable music in combination with the sounds, rather than the sights, of their environments. It is now appropriate to review Connor's discussion. He refers to the musical aesthetics of John Cage and also, of particular relevance to this study, discusses the Walkman. He writes:

> In the Walkman we have a perfectly ordinary and very casual coming together of the impulse towards absolute technical perfection that we find in CD technology, in which what we hear has never taken place in the here and now—it's a purely artificial sound—and the aesthetics of John Cage, who wanted music to be an exposure to the here and now, to the chances of what happens to happen ... (1999:308)

Connor observes that mobile listeners hear the combination of two sets of sounds: their portable music with ambient environmental noises. It is already noted, particularly in the introduction and in the discussion of chosen sounds, that portable music is the listener's choice of listening material. Portable music's status as the fulfillment of the listener's desire to hear it is of greater relevance to this discussion than Connor's implied criticism of its artificiality. Nonetheless, the keenness of Connor's observations and the perceptive connection he draws between the sounds of portable music and Cage's musical aesthetics provide a key to understanding aestheticisation's second mode. He notes that Cage's aesthetics provide a theoretical framework within which ambient environmental noise is considered of aesthetic or artistic significance. These aesthetics are exemplified in Cage's infamous 1952 piece, *4' 33"*, in which the performer makes no sounds. This work is considered to epitomise chance in composition and indeterminacy in performance because the only sounds an audience hears for its duration are random ambient environmental noises. In effect, in *4' 33"*, Cage '... simply invites audiences to listen to the sounds around them ...' (Nicholls 2002:228). Related to the functions of portable music, Connor suggests that, combined with a listener's chosen portable music, ambient sounds can provide an enjoyable listening experience. Mobile listening becomes partially predetermined and partially indeterminate and listeners enjoy it for the chance juxtaposition of their chosen sounds with random environmental noises.

Connor also discusses mobile listeners' interactions with their environments and responds to a common abuse of the Walkman—that is, '... it seems to subtract people from social life' (1999:308). By contrast, Connor suggests that:

> ... the experience of the Walkman, the intoxication of the Walkman, comes from the fact that for the user they're not withdrawn from the scene that they're walking through or the tube train that they're sitting in. The Walkman-user is often creating a kind of a chance collage between the sounds that are filtering through and are purely contingent and the organized sound that they're hearing. (1999:308)

Connor's 'chance collage' exemplifies aestheticisation's second mode. Furthermore, Connor clearly believes the experience of listening to portable music in public is not solitary. Listeners are engaged with their environments, noticing aspects that are pleasing in combination with their portable music. In sum, aestheticisation involves the listener's surroundings. The listener's surroundings, in turn, are irrefutable evidence of the listener's place within a collective and social environment.

In her interview Aliese discussed an example of aestheticisation's second mode. She recounted:

> One day I was waiting for someone at the Silver Balls[1] and I was listening to my Walkman. I think I was listening to the Spice Girls but there was a guy playing the violin and the violin line fit really well with whatever the Spice Girls were doing. I was just thinking, "This is really cool, I wish this guy could hear it, like he should play this [Spice Girls recording] as he is going". (2001)

Aliese hears her portable music as it combines with the noises of her environment. In this case, Aliese's portable music combines with other sounds widely regarded as musical – the playing of a busker violinist. It is not necessary, however, that the ambient noises in aestheticisation be of this nature. Listeners can enjoy any type of ambient sound in combination with their portable music. Listeners, as discussed above, can also enjoy the combination of their portable music with the sights of their surroundings and transform their daily journeys through otherwise unremarkable environments.

Function Four: Environmental Control

In environmental control, listeners use portable music to replace external sounds they consider unpleasant. As a result, listeners perceive portable music rather than ambient sounds to be their sonic environment or soundscape.

Intuitively, aestheticisation and environmental control appear to be similar. Note that in aestheticisation portable music is the replacement 'soundtrack' of the listener's aestheticised experience of the surrounding environment. In environmental control, portable music is a replacement 'soundscape' for the listener's surrounding environment. The difference between a soundscape (portable music's role in environmental control) and a soundtrack (portable music's role in aestheticisation) defines the essential difference, as well as any perceived similarity, between the two functions.

The literature features several accounts of listeners' use of recorded music other than portable music to control soundscapes. First, Eisenberg draws a distinction between the act of listening to recorded music on the one hand, and using it to control the sonic environment on the other. He writes:

> The city is no place for *listening* to records. Half the time one has to use them as shields against other people's sounds. Music becomes a substitute for silence. (1988:44, italics in original)

Eisenberg believes the use of recorded music as a shield against the noises of other people is distinct from listening to records for the sake of the music. That is, people who use music to block out other noises do not listen to it in any concentrated fashion. However, this study's interviews reveal contrasting points of view. For example, Miriam compared her Walkman to her household stereo as a means of listening to recorded music:

> ... often, even if I'm in bed, I'll just pop the Discman on anyway, just because it sort of blocks out a bit more of the noise [than the stereo does] so that you can actually concentrate fully on what you're hearing.[2] (2001)

Unlike Eisenberg, Miriam draws no distinction between concentrated listening and the use of recorded music to block out ambient noise, feeling that recorded music's ability to overcome external noise actually complements its use as the focus of

•CHAPTER THREE•   29

concentrated listening. Aaron, a violinist, described his mobile listening similarly:

> It [the Walkman] forces you to concentrate on what you're listening to a bit more. It's right in your ear. I use it if I'm preparing new works, reading the score as I'm listening. Before I go to bed one of my favourite pastimes is to choose a CD or particular piece that I'm interested in listening to in depth with no outside stimulus at all, turn off the lights, lie down and basically have just the sound. There's no other distraction and I find that I get a lot out of that. (2001)

Aaron's portable music blocks out external noises and, together with the elimination of visual stimuli and distractions, this enhances his ability to concentrate on the music. In contrast to the sharp distinction Eisenberg draws between listening to music and using it to block out unwanted ambient noise, Aaron and Miriam recognised the reduction in ambient noise associated with listening to portable music as an aid to their ability to focus on the music. In the terminology of this study, Miriam's and Aaron's interview responses illustrate how environmental control complements chosen sounds and the way the two functions take place concurrently.

Sean Cubitt discusses a particular feature of recorded music that contributes to its capacity to control listeners' sonic environments. He writes:

> Recording is ... a way of controlling the soundscape so that it will always conform to an already catalogued expectation, magically confirming our desire to hear with the desired sound. (1998:100)

The repetition inherent to recorded music—the music is the same each time the recording is played—means listeners know exactly what they will hear when they play a recording and thus exactly what recorded soundscape will replace nondesired external sounds. To Cubitt, this foreknowledge is an inherent part of the control that recorded music allows listeners to impose over their sonic environments. This principle was confirmed by Lorrin in her interview, when she recounted:

> When I'm using my computer to work, I put a CD in the tray and put the earphones in, turn it up fairly loud and listen to music that I'm familiar with so I can drown out the sound of everyone else in the office and concentrate on my work. I'm more productive because there's other things happening in

the office and I don't hear conversations which, if I didn't have the headphones on, I would probably join in and stop working. (2001)

This is a straightforward account of environmental control in which Lorrin's portable music enables her to manage her sonic environment in order to work more productively. Lorrin's use of familiar music supports Cubitt's suggestion that repetition enhances recorded music's capacity to control environmental sounds for listeners. Nonetheless, for some writers, recorded music's repetition is problematic. It is now appropriate to review this aspect of the experience of recorded music.

Repetition

Roger Sessions holds particularly strong opinions regarding recorded music's repetition. He recalls:

> ... the day, some fifteen years previously, when I had hurled a gramophone record across the room in a fury, intentionally shattering it. I did this not because it was a bad recording or a bad performance or even a bad piece. It was none of these things; it was Debussy's *Fêtes*, beautifully played by, I think, the Philadelphia Orchestra. I loved the piece, and still love it. But what infuriated me was my fully-developed awareness of having heard exactly the same sounds, exactly the same nuances, both of tempo and dynamics, the same accents, down to the minutest detail, so many times that I knew exactly—and I emphasize *exactly*, to the last instant—what was coming next. The performance of the music had become, as regards my awareness of it, completely mechanical, and I reacted as one does to any sensation of mechanical repetition. (1970:52, italics in original)

In later writing, Sessions explains his violent reaction to literal repetition in music. He proposes that recorded music holds pleasure for listeners as long as it remains to some degree unfamiliar. It is likely to be of no further interest the instant the listener becomes aware of literal repetition (Daniel Boorstin [see 1974:385] expresses a similar view). Sessions' assertions invite comparisons between recorded and live music, and Sessions is not alone in criticising the repetitious aspect of recorded music, especially as it stands in comparison with live music's inevitable variation. For example, Bartók also contributes to this discourse and imagines a time when, in terms of fidelity, '... the reproduced music will necessarily be exactly the same as the live music ...' (1976:298). Bartók then asserts:

> But even in that case there will be an irreplaceable superiority, for which there is no substitute, of the live music over the stored, canned music. This substitute is the variability of live music. That which lives changes from moment to moment; music recorded by machines hardens into something stationary. (1976:298)

Live music is inherently variable; even repeated performances of a given work by the same ensemble in a given venue inevitably differ to some extent. Conversely, recorded music is identical each time it is played. Thus, while Cubitt feels recorded music's repetition enhances its functionality for listeners such as Lorrin, who uses it to control her aural environment, Sessions feels, because of repetition, recorded music sometimes even '... ceases to be music' (1971:71).

Lee Brown rejects Sessions' milder assertion, noted above, that recorded music is no longer interesting for listeners the instant they become aware of repetition in the details of its interpretation. He argues that there are three mechanisms by which the repeated experience of recorded music remains musically interesting (see 2000a:113–119), although it is his conclusions that are most relevant to this argument. He writes:

> ... we listen to sound recordings as documents of an art form that is more and more *constituted* by the medium, in the sense that our experience of the thing as it is documented is something very different from our experience of it in its live, never-to-be-repeated state. (2000a:123, italics in original)

As noted in Chapter One, Brown advocates the study of recorded music on the basis that it differs markedly from live music. Also noted in Chapter One, Berland suggests that the meaning of music depends on the means of its transmission and therefore that recorded music's meanings can differ from those of live music. Brown and Berland imply that judging of recorded music on criteria applicable only to live music is dubious. Sessions' criticism of recordings on the basis of their lack of interpretive variation is an example of a judgment of recorded music that Brown and Berland might view with scepticism. Furthermore, Lorrin's interview suggests Brown's and Berland's views resonate with at least some mobile listeners who enjoy and take advantage of recorded music's repetition. Such listeners know their portable music and enjoy a listening experience that precisely conforms to their expectations. This is not to deny the validity of opinions such as Sessions', because different listeners have different expectations of their listening experience. It is undeniable, however, that the experiences of live music and recorded music are different. It is foolish to expect live music to exactly fulfill every preconceived expectation in the manner of recorded music, just as it is foolish to demand variation from recorded music in the manner of live music.

Adorno also discusses the inherent repetition of recorded music, writing:

> There is no doubt that, as music is removed by the phonograph record from the realm of live production and from the imperative of artistic activity and becomes petrified, it absorbs into itself, in this process of petrification, the very life that would otherwise vanish. The dead art rescues the ephemeral and perishing art as the only one alive. Therein may lie the phonograph record's most profound justification, which cannot be impugned by an aesthetic objection to its reification. (Adorno 1990b:59)

A musical performance, normally evanescent, is rescued by its recording. It is captured and preserved, to be heard again each time the recording is played. Adorno observes, though, that this rescue comes at the price of the music's '... third dimension: its height and its abyss' (1990b:57). Adorno's reference to music's 'third dimension', originally written in 1934, anticipates Benjamin's 1935 discussion of the 'aura' of the work of art in "The Work of Art in the Age of Mechanical Reproduction (published in English in 1968). By 'third dimension' Adorno means the interpretive variation inherent to live music. This differs slightly from Benjamin's 'aura', which refers to the uniqueness of original, nonreproduced, artworks. Both writers regret the lack of interpretive variation in recordings, the qualities which tie live performances to their place and time and make them unique. Unlike Sessions, however, Adorno feels the recording's 'rescue' of otherwise ephemeral music justifies the loss of interpretive variation. This is perhaps the ultimate justification for recording music. It goes beyond Cubitt's justification on the grounds that recorded music sets listeners' expectations and then is the only means by which those expectations can subsequently be filled. Although it is now considered commonplace and often taken for granted, recording is a significant development in the experience of music and it is unrealistic to expect that recordings should overcome music's ephemeral nature while maintaining interpretive variation.

Mobile listeners use portable music to control their sonic environments, environments occupied by people as well as by inanimate sources of sound. Such listening consequently impacts on listeners' interactions with other people. Several writers discuss the social consequences of the use of portable music in environmental control, although they do not use this study's terminology. These discussions are reviewed below; however, it is appropriate to first examine one of this study's interview responses. David's mobile listening exemplifies the way portable music, used by listeners in environmental control, modifies personal interaction. He recounts:

> In the past I have done a lot of 3D-CAD[3] work. It is a very single minded task at times and sometimes repetitive and often requires extended periods of model regeneration time. Listening to a CD through earphones blocks out all the background noise: other people's chatter and phone conversation, machinery noise etc. It allows you to "zone out". (2001)

David eliminates the noises of his workmates by listening to portable music. The noise of their conversations might otherwise tempt him to interact but David's mobile listening eliminates the potential for this distraction and demonstrates possible social side effects of environmental control.

Hosokawa examines the effect illustrated above. He introduces the concept of *musica mobilis* and defines it '... as music whose source voluntarily or involuntarily moves from one point to another, coordinated by the corporal transportation of the source owner(s)' (1984:166). Hosokawa describes the development of *musica mobilis* as four stages in the evolving interactions between people involved in playing and hearing music. Each stage accompanies a technological advance in sound production and the last is facilitated by the Walkman. In Hosokawa's first stage, the relevant sound is '... the tone of urban life in general' and '... nothing but one of the secondary consequences of other non-music-making activities ...' which occur as people move around the city. Interaction involving such sound '... only shows that those involved *live together*' (1984:166, italics in original). An example is interaction that takes place between a vendor and a buyer to the sound of the vendor's cries. The second stage involves the sounds of street musicians who play in the urban setting to earn money. Hosokawa notes:

> Though the music is transmitted mono-directionally, the two groups [musicians and audience] react and "communicate" bi-directionally: a mutual tuning-in relation is maintained even if it is very transitory. (1984:167)

Hosokawa describes the interpersonal relations in the second stage as '... *making-music-together* ...' (1984:167, italics in original). In the third stage people do not play music or even create it as part of their daily activities. Rather, they '... listen to it [recorded music] through technological "instruments"' as they move through the city. As examples of this practice, Hosokawa discusses people who listen to portable radios, cassette players or car stereo systems. He observes that a form of interaction still occurs as listeners walk or drive through the city with their technological instruments dispersing music because 'Passers-by are obliged to hear it for a few seconds'. Hosokawa terms the interaction that results '... *listening-to-the-music-together*' (1984:167, italics in original).

The final stage in the development of *musica mobilis* is manifest in '... the walkman listener, who is found in the world of *listening to music alone*' (1984:167, italics in original). In an example of environmental control, Hosokawa suggests that the '... listener seems to cut the auditory contact with the outer world where he really lives: seeking the perfection of his "individual" zone of listening ...' (1984:167). Hosokawa's discussion describes his understanding of the historical lineage of Walkman-related behaviour and also how the behaviour of mobile listeners relates to the social fabric surrounding them. Hosokawa believes mobile listening is inherently an act of solipsism. Listeners dismiss the auditory content of their environment, including that essential for social interaction, preferring instead their own chosen soundscapes, transmitted directly to their ears by their mobile listening devices. Thus, with regard to environmental control, Hosokawa feels the act of mobile listening is a rejection of social interaction, achieved by listeners as they eliminate ambient sounds.

Chambers also discusses mobile listening and, in doing so, illuminates a social aspect to what often is considered, in the mode of Hosokawa, a solitary experience. Focusing on the experiences of individual listeners, Chambers sees mobile listeners as occupying an '... ambiguous position ...' '... between autism and autonomy ...' (1994:51). The autistic condition is one of self-absorption and a reduced ability to respond to or communicate with the outside world (Rey Chow [1999:475] also discusses mobile listening in terms of autism). By comparison, the state of autonomy is one of personal freedom. In positioning the mobile listening experience ambiguously between these two conditions, Chambers suggests that autonomy, the goal of many mobile listeners, is only achieved at the cost of 'autistic' interactions with the outside world. Listeners cannot cut themselves off from the sounds of their environments and still participate in normal social interaction. Unlike Hosokawa, Chambers feels that mobile listeners' dismissal of their environments is not complete. Observing a contradiction in mobile listeners' actions, he proposes that 'Each listener/player selects and rearranges the surrounding soundscape, and, in constructing a dialogue with it, leaves a trace in the network' (1994:50). Chambers' observation (that listeners select and rearrange their soundscapes) points directly to the discussion of environmental control. Chambers also uses the term 'dialogue'. This suggests a two-way communication and implies that mobile listeners, despite their apparent isolation, are actually engaged with their environments. Chambers subsequently makes this explicit when he writes 'In the manifest refusal of sociability the Walkman nevertheless reaffirms participation in a shared environment' (1994:50). In environmental control, mobile listeners employ portable music in response to their environments. Chambers suggests the fundamentally reactionary nature of these strategies only confirms listeners' reluctant, and thus autistic or maladjusted, involvement in their environments, as opposed to the autonomy they aim to achieve.

Like Chambers, Chow also suggests mobile listening is not without a social component. Chow's understanding of the social participation she observes involving mobile listeners differs, however, from that of Chambers and also Hosokawa. As noted, Chambers and Hosokawa discuss mobile listening in terms of listeners' withdrawal from their surroundings, even if, in Chambers' estimation, listeners' withdrawal only reconfirms their essential participation in those environments. By comparison, Chow discusses mobile listening in terms of listeners' subversion of the powers authorities hold over them, writing that mobile listening can be '... a "silent" sabotage of the technology of collectivization with its own instruments' (1999:475) and hence a form of social or even political action. Before mounting her argument Chow refers to Adorno's description of popular music in America as '... a training course in a passivity that will probably spread to his [the fan's] thought and social conduct' (1976:30). Chow states her belief that mobile listeners are actively engaged with their environments, rather then withdrawing from them. Then, explaining her understanding of the mobile listener's subversion of the regimes to which they are subject, suggests that, because portable music is hidden from others, it '... leads to a certain freedom. This is the freedom to be deaf to the loudspeakers of history ...' (1999:475). It should be noted that Chow writes with regard to communist China, where propaganda is transmitted by means of loudspeakers. Tetsuo also notes loudspeakers are a component of ambient noise that mobile listeners seek to avoid, writing "one gains protection from the more and more electronics-oriented city environment with blaring speakers, noisy traffic and flickering shop windows" (1988:60). In environmental control, portable music screens out these sounds and also makes it impossible for bystanders to share or understand listeners' experiences. Thus portable music provides:

> ... the possibility of a barrier, a blockage between "me" and the world, so that, as in moments of undisturbed sleep, I can disappear as a listener playing music. (Chow 1999:475)

In this manner mobile listeners withdraw from the regimes to which they are subject, effectively rendering the regimes impotent. The social aspect of this apparently solitary experience is clarified when Chow writes '... the Walkman's artificiality makes us aware of the impending presence of the collective ...' (1999:475). For Chow, the Walkman's artificiality is the listener's impression of their absence from the collective. This impression is, of course, deceptive, and in this aspect Chow's argument is reminiscent of Chambers' assertion, cited above, that mobile listeners cannot completely exclude their surroundings.

Regina Bendix also observes the paradox between mobile listeners' apparent withdrawal from their surroundings and the social consequences of this reactionary behaviour. Reviewing Bull's studies, she observes that:

> ... the social collective does not disappear in this personal maneuvering [listening to Walkman Music to block out environmental noises] on the part of the individual. At any moment, forces beyond the individual can intrude on the carefully managed aesthetic and experiential control, and the very fragility of this strategy thus continually reminds the individual of the powers—social and technological—that control her environment. (2000:38)

It is notable that Bendix, Chambers, and Chow all make this point. Each writer suggests that mobile listeners' attempts to block out their environment only confirm their presence in its midst. Hosokawa does not acknowledge this paradox, suggesting mobile listeners are successful in cutting contact with their environments. Of the writers reviewed here, he is the most concerned regarding the social consequences of this severance, suggesting that mobile listening is the most recent of a number of steps of decreasing social interaction which are a consequence of music's ever increasing transmission by recording rather than live performance. Although Hosokawa differs from Bendix, Chambers, and Chow regarding the effectiveness with which mobile listeners cut themselves off from their surroundings, both sides of the argument acknowledge that listeners control their environments with portable music, replacing ambient sonic environments, including noises related to social interaction, with their preferred sounds.

Many personal accounts of mobile listening are found in the literature and a high proportion of them demonstrate environmental control. These sources, along with personal accounts from the interviews, serve to highlight different aspects of mobile listeners' experiences of the function. Bull discusses mobile listeners' motivations, writing:

> Users might be aiming to block out any external sound that they might otherwise hear in the street or elsewhere. The intrusion of any collection of aural sounds located within space is unwanted. They aim, through use, to replace the involuntary auditory sounds experienced in public space by their own personal soundscape placed directly between their ears. (2000:186)

Also clearly pertinent to discussion of environmental control, Lind comments that '... the personal stereo allows the user to alter any acoustical environment' (1989:6). Williamson similarly observes:

> It [the Walkman] attempts to negate *chance*: you never know what you are going to hear on a bus or on the streets, but the walk-person is buffered against the unexpected—an apparent triumph of individual control over social spontaneity. (1988:210, italics in original)

Williamson's discussion relates especially to the *control* aspect of environmental control and concludes that portable music represents listeners' implementation of personally selected constraints over the random nature of their aural environments. Chambers also puts this idea forward, writing:

> ... if the Walkman so far represents the ultimate form of the art of the transit, it also represents the ultimate musical means in mediating the ambient. For it permits the possibility, however fragile and however transitory, of

imposing your soundscape on the surrounding aural environment and thereby domesticating the external world: for a moment it can all be brought under the STOP/START, FAST FORWARD, PAUSE and REWIND buttons. (1994:51, capitalisation in original)

Chambers extends discussion of environmental control beyond the idea of portable music simply as a replacement soundscape. He understands portable music to act in this way, but proposes that such replacement provides a means by which listeners tame what they perceive as a hostile external environment. Chambers thus proposes that, by controlling their environments, listeners can influence their feelings and render themselves comfortable in many different, and sometimes oppressive, environments.

Moebius and Michel-Annen, as discussed in the Introduction, analyse mobile listening based on listeners' varying interactions with their environments. They use the term 'everyday' to describe listeners' environments and propose that portable music changes listeners' interactions with those environments. Describing these interactions from the listener's point of view, they write:

This appliance mediates a hitherto unknown intensity of hearing: everyday sound, the environmental noise, is suppressed. Walkman users feel the music as if it were inside them. There is no localized source of sound, no big loudspeakers, no instrumentalist. The music appears to be directly in their head, and attains a consciousness-filling quality. The sense of hearing is flooded with music, and normal communication may become well-nigh impossible. Contact with the environment, then, takes place through the eyes, not the ears. The meaning of vision increases from the subjective point of view of the Walkman user. (1994:572)

This is an evocative description of listening to portable music and an excellent account of environmental control. It highlights the significance of headphones to the experience of environmental control as mobile listeners 'inject' portable music directly into the ears, flooding them with musical sensation and eliminating ambient noises from their experience.

It is interesting to note the contrast between Moebius' and Michel-Annen's account of mobile listening and those discussed earlier relating to aestheticisation. In aestheticisation, the listener experiences a collage or combination of portable music and their environment. By contrast, Moebius and Michel-Annen describe a separation along the lines of the senses; portable music floods the hearing while interactions with the surroundings are conducted visually. Moebius and Michel-Annen regard these different aspects of mobile listening as separate, even though they are concurrent.

The final relevant source in the literature is from the anonymous writer for *The New Yorker*, already reviewed in relation to aestheticisation, who gives an evocative account of her own experience in which portable music functions as a means of environmental control. She writes:

> I know how people who don't wear Walkmen feel about the rest of us. I know because of the way they ask me if I think it's such a good idea to wear headphones around, as if there might be something *natural* or *wholesome* about subjecting oneself to the cacophony of, say, a midtown sidewalk next to a construction site during rush hour. Once in a while, when my batteries run low, I'm forced to hear what I've been missing, and, except for the occasional titillating snatch of conversation, I don't think it amounts to much.[4] (Anon. 1989:19–20, italics in original)

This mobile listener uses portable music because she considers it more interesting and less offensive than ambient noise. Along with the sources cited above, this description of the experience of portable music conveys the essence of environmental control, in which the convenience of portable music enables listeners to modify their experiences of their aural environments wherever and whenever they choose.

In addition to the literature cited above, several of this study's interviewees recounted mobile listening related to environmental control. Like David and Lorrin, whose ideas are cited above, Fiona also listens at work. She recounted:

> I use headphones at work to listen to music via my CD-ROM player. As I work in an open plan office it is sometimes hard to concentrate with the level of noise around me. (2001)

Fiona listens to portable music at work to eliminate ambient noise and thus optimise her ability to concentrate on her duties. Jessica similarly described her listening as an escape from ambient noise although, by contrast, Jessica's listening is not intended to improve her productivity, but simply to eliminate sounds she describes as boring:

> All you can hear walking around the city is shops advertising themselves and people talking and it's not stuff that I haven't heard before. So it's not something that I miss out on and they're easy to take out [by listening to portable music]. (2001)

Jessica considers ambient noise to be boring rather than unpleasant in the sense of a violent assault on her hearing. Using portable music as a replacement soundscape enables her to overcome the monotony to which she would otherwise be subject as she moves through the city. These are obvious examples of environmental control in that the listeners use portable music in order to avoid the sounds of their environments. However, in the finer details of listeners' motivations, these accounts vary slightly from others already discussed. For example, Williamson, as noted above, suggests listeners choose to control their own sonic environments as an exercise in overcoming the vagaries of chance or in order to feel rebellious. Hosokawa, also noted above, suggests environmental control is really a side effect of listeners' pursuit of their own 'perfect' listening experience. By contrast, both the *New Yorker* writer and Jessica argue that ambient noise is mundane, even unnatural, by comparison with their chosen music and better avoided as a result. Fiona's, David's, and Lorrin's listening represent their attempts to be productive in their workplaces. Miriam's and Aaron's listening reflects their desire to listen to their chosen music without distraction. Despite the slight variations in motivation, these accounts of mobile listening each epitomise environmental control: listeners' control of their aural environments with portable music.

At this point, having examined literature and fieldwork results that demonstrate how listeners employ portable music as environmental control, it is pertinent to highlight the interview responses of one particular mobile listener. Steven's response contrasted with the discourse reviewed above and with every other interview related to environmental control. He described his response to the purchase of a minidisc recording Walkman in a lengthy e-mail:

> I never intended to use it as a Walkman (it was for field-recordings mostly, as I am occasionally guilty of contributing to the glut of experimental electronic noise myself) but since I had this portable music listening device I slowly got into the habit of (very) carefully taking it along for the daily commute. I think about the time that I started doing this I was infatuated with this particular CD which was mostly atmospheric drone. As you can imagine, this didn't come across very well on public transport [because of its resemblance to ambient noise], but I persisted for a little while. I noticed that my listening tastes were slowly propagating towards beats [dance music] again to defeat the restrictions of my primary listening situation. I noticed this trend and I wasn't too happy about it. I didn't like the idea of such an arbitrary external force moulding my musical taste. I battled against it for a while, even purchasing some noise-cancelling headphones at one

point, but they really don't provide the absolute silence required to enjoy some of the CDs which I was listening to at the time. This led to me discarding the whole idea of personal audio in exchange for a more developed appreciation of ambient noise. It hit home when I was deciding if I should take my minidisc on holiday with me. Surely there would be things to hear as well as things to see? This made me wonder how much of a waste it would be to block out the sound around me as habit. Would you wander around with your eyes closed if it were technically feasible? What makes vision more interesting than sound? It's even more likely that I will hear something interesting on any given day than it is that I will see something interesting. (2001)

Steven composes experimental electronic music and it is possible this pursuit is related to a heightened sensitivity to sound on his part. Perhaps for this reason, Steven's response is at odds others examined in this study regarding environmental control; it bears closer examination for this reason. Steven's thoughts are triggered by his enjoyment of a recording that resembles ambient noise. When he attempts to listen to this recording on public transport the high noise levels overwhelm it. When Steven subsequently finds himself listening to other recordings that feature more highly defined musical events he is displeased that his musical preferences are at the mercy of external and arbitrary forces. When Steven is considering whether or not to take his Walkman on holiday with him, he realises that blocking out the sounds of his holiday and listening instead to portable music essentially defeats the purpose of his holiday. By listening to portable music, Steven feels he would be wasting an opportunity for new experiences. Steven draws a telling comparison, observing the fatuity of wilfully controlling the visual content of his holiday. On consideration, Steven decides to develop a heightened appreciation of ambient noise, reminiscent of the musical aesthetics of John Cage, as discussed above. No prediction can be made regarding the frequency of opinions like Steven's in the broader population, but his ideas are noteworthy and demonstrate that the literature most certainly does not capture every nuance of musical experience.

Function Five: Boundary Demarcation

In boundary demarcation, mobile listeners feel that portable music sets them apart from their surroundings, 'removing' them from unpleasant environments. Listeners have this perception as a result of portable music's dual capacity to engage their attention and to block out ambient noise.

The literature features several discussions of listeners' use of music to set themselves apart from their surroundings. First, Gumpert develops the concepts of 'acoustical space' and 'the wall of sound' to discuss music's establishment of boundaries between listeners and their surroundings. He defines the wall of sound as '... that sense of acoustical space which surrounds each of us ...' (1987:87) and suggests that the acoustic maintenance of personal space is a practice whose origins lie in audible signals generated by animals as a means of marking their territory. The cricket song is an example of this and Gumpert suggests that music, especially recorded music, provides humans with a similar capacity. As Gumpert observes:

> Many of us surround and protect ourselves with walls of sound while we are engaged in public activity. A bicycle is adorned with a small radio. A picnic includes a portable radio in the spread. The distance between blankets on a crowded day at the beach is not only determined by personal space, but by zones of music. (1987:87)

Gumpert's discussion indicates precedence for boundary demarcation in forms of recorded music other than portable music, and suggests music can demarcate a boundary around groups as well as around individual listeners. Following Gumpert's observations, it seems that boundary demarcation's origins lie in fundamental responses to sound and music. The development of devices such as the Walkman and iPod allows listeners to take advantage of this territory-defining capacity of music wherever and whenever they feel the need. Gumpert offers further pertinent insights, writing:

> While the speakers of a portable radio or cassette player create a wall of amplified sound, earphones and earplugs create a silent wall, which separates the listener from those around him or her. The earphone mentality is based on privatization and isolation—on withdrawal from public sound and interaction. For some, like the roller skater or the music aficionado, excluding the extraneous helps them concentrate. For commuters, the motive is to create another sound environment, replacing the one which accompanies the mundane, routinized ritual, or to substitute pleasant sound for often harmful noise. (1987:89–90)

Gumpert suggests that there might be many deeper motivations behind listeners' use of boundary demarcation—a particular single function of portable music.

•CHAPTER THREE•

To briefly digress, Chanan also examines the Walkman and observes a particular combined effect of stereo music recording and headphones, which adds to portable music's capacity to define personal space. He writes:

> Headphones allowed the listener to attach their head directly to the source of the sound, dissolving the physical space of their body into the virtual space created by the music's stereo image. (1995:154)

'Stereo image' is a phenomenon associated with stereo recordings in which two channels are independently recorded and played back. Listeners perceive the effect of sound coming from different directions in three-dimensional space, apparently larger than the real space defined by their headphones. Chanan attributes the capacity of portable music to create a virtual space to its stereo image, suggesting listeners understand their music's stereo image to correspond to their own personal space.

To return to Gumpert, in the terminology of this study, he understands boundary demarcation to be an extension of environmental control. This is apparent in his references, cited above, to '... excluding the extraneous ...' and to commuters' creation of '... another sound environment ...', clear examples of environmental control. Most importantly with regard to boundary demarcation, note that Gumpert's discussion regarding the '... earphones and earplugs ...' continues his discussion of the wall of sound. This illustrates that, as noted, boundary demarcation is simply a more recent manifestation, possible since the rise of mobile listening, of a property that sound and music have always possessed.

Several interview responses support Gumpert's ideas. First, Darryl's account of his mobile listening on daily train commutes between his home and work corresponds with Gumpert's observations relating to the acoustic creation and maintenance of personal space. He observes:

> I think there's so many people on the train and everyone's after their own personal space. I reckon it gives you your own personal space if you've got your Walkman on. (2001)

Then, summarising his mobile listening and making the role of portable music in this function clear, Darryl recounted:

> It's just that it's my own personal space. A lot of the times I just go into my own world, like totally zone out, and I can think about all sorts of things or think about nothing apart from just thinking about the music. (2001)

Darryl uses the idea of his personal space to explain his mobile listening. It is useful to compare Darryl's account of his listening with Gumpert's suggestion that earphones and earplugs demarcate boundaries for listeners. Darryl states that, while listening, he might think only about his music. This statement implies that Darryl's portable music, and particularly his focused concentration on it, allows him to create personal space in a crowded environment. Darryl's earphones, which transmit portable music directly to his ears and block ambient noise in the manner of environmental control, also play a role. Ultimately though, it is Darryl's portable music and his concentration on it that results in his feelings of personal space and his experience of boundary demarcation.

Darryl's idea of personal space recurs in interviewees' understandings of their mobile listening, although various respondents use different terminology. Ellen expressed these sentiments in different words, saying:

> ... you're in your own little world when you're listening to the Walkman. (2001)

Ellen's concept of her '... own little world ...' corresponds to a personal space, although Ellen's expression captures her state of mind while listening as well as the space that literally surrounds her. Her thoughts are directed toward the music rather than to her surroundings. Scott, although not using the term 'personal space', nonetheless also explains his listening to portable music in terms of a 'space':

> I prefer listening to the Walkman on the bus than not having the Walkman. It puts me into a space that isn't on the bus and I just kind of escape with it. (2001)

When asked to describe his understanding of the space he experiences, Scott responds:

> It's another place, another dimension I guess. I'm not on the bus when I'm listening to the music. I'm somewhere else. I'm listening to the band or in the band. I'm not there. (2001)

Scott relates the space he perceives to the experience of live music as part of the audience or as a band member. This is a particular example of the listener's 'removal' from their surroundings and Scott states that, for him, this phenomenon is not peculiar to portable music:

> I get that on a stereo as well. But I think it's also the context, that I'm on the bus and it's boring on the bus so I'm more likely to do it there. (2001)

Scott's statement, acknowledging he is 'somewhere else' when listening to music on a stereo, serves to reiterate an important point regarding boundary demarcation. This function of portable music is a recent manifestation, possible since the development of the Walkman and iPod, of listener's responses to previous forms of music, live and recorded, and to sound in general. As noted, portable listening devices such as the Walkman and iPod simply allow listeners to take advantage of music's capacities to define territory wherever and whenever they desire.

Berland discusses the nature of the boundary that listeners consider recorded music to demarcate around them. She observes:

> We objectify location as the space that contains our individual means of reception: the car, bedroom, or bar where the music is heard, the physical site within which one's body is surrounded by sound. (1998:130)

Listeners 'objectify' their location as the place defined by the music they hear there; that is, music can define boundaries in the manner of walls and other physical barriers. The examples that Berland provides of the car, bedroom, and bar, where music other than portable music achieves this objectification, are examples of precursors to boundary demarcation. However, in actual instances of boundary demarcation involving portable music, the listener's 'location' is not so easily defined because its boundaries do not coincide with easily observable physical boundaries. Portable music is transmitted to single listeners by headphones and listeners hear it wherever they happen to be. By Berland's analysis, listeners are 'located' in the space within which their '... body is surrounded by sound' (1998:130). It is clear that mobile listeners' bodies are not surrounded by sound in the sense that the bodies of other, non-headphone using, music listeners are surrounded. Nonetheless, the headphones inherent to portable music can give listeners the impression that their portable music surrounds them, leading to the objectification of location that Berland discusses.

Davies draws a distinction between listening to recorded music and its use by listeners in order to 'withdraw' from their surroundings. He first notes the benefits for listeners of recorded music over live music, observing that, with recorded music, listeners can hear what they like, when and where they like and while doing what they like (see 2001b:327–328). Davies then notes that, as a result, the listener '... can cocoon herself in sound for much of her waking life' (2001b:328). Such use of recorded music relates to boundary demarcation and Davies' use of the word 'cocoon' evokes some of the sense of listeners' experience of this function. Davies asserts that an associated consequence of this use of recorded music is that the music '... is liable to slip below the horizon of consciousness' (2001b:330) and that listeners '... treat music as not requiring ... attention' (2001b:330). He refers to this as the 'desensitization' (2001b:330) of listeners and makes it clear he considers the desensitised consumption of music, as opposed to really listening to it, a regrettable consequence of music's recording. The distinction that Davies draws between listening to music and using it to demarcate a boundary is reminiscent of Eisenberg's thoughts, reviewed above as they pertain to environmental control. As noted, Eisenberg draws a distinction between the act of listening to recorded music on the one hand and using it to control the sonic environment on the other, although this study's interviews revealed contrasting points of view. The interviewees suggested portable music's capacity to eliminate ambient noises complements its use as the focus of a concentrated listening experience. Similarly, the interviews inform discussion of Davies' views as they relate to boundary demarcation. For example, Shoji stated:

> Sometimes it [listening to portable music] is very good for not being distracted when there's all sorts of things going on around me like people saying disgusting things and all sorts of stuff. If you want to remain focussed it's a bit easier. (2001)

Shoji listens to portable music because it isolates him from his working environment and he consequently feels his concentration on his work improves. It is noteworthy that Shoji's concentration is not directed toward his portable music but toward his work. In Davies' (2001b:330) terminology, Shoji is 'desensitised' toward the music which serves to establish a boundary between his surroundings and himself. Shoji's listening supports Davies' theory.

It is also pertinent to consider the subtext to Davies' observations; namely, that it is regrettable music is used to demarcate a boundary rather than for focused listening. This study's fieldwork results also offer insight into this discussion. Lorrin listens to portable music at work '... to block out sound ...' and '... to enjoy the music' (2001). In her interview she recounted:

> When I am working I am concentrating on the task at hand and not the music but when I finish that task I often then listen and enjoy the music. Therefore it is playing without my noticing it. Is this unfortunate? I guess in a way but I don't appreciate the music any less as a result. Am I disrespecting the intent of the artist? Probably, but I don't think this is a result of having a recording of the music. Even at a live concert I find my attention will occasionally wane. I start thinking about something else and I am no longer hearing the music. Whether it is due to a lack of concentration or preoccupation with another task I think that music will always become background noise at some time. Even if my exposure to music is reduced there will still be times when I am not listening, as unfortunate as it may seem. (2001)

At work, Lorrin's attention is not always focused on the music she is hearing. At times she may be distracted by tasks at hand. Lorrin maintains that the variations in her concentration are not necessarily related to the fact that she is listening to recorded music, because her concentration also wavers at live concerts. Lorrin's distraction at concerts does not contradict the connection that Davies draws between increased exposure to music as a result of recording and desensitised consumption; Lorrin might not find herself distracted a live concerts if she did not hear as much music as recordings enable her to. Davies' argument against recorded music mainly concerns the overexposure he observes as a result of recording rather than the phenomenon of recording itself. Lorrin perceives that her occasionally distracted listening may not be ideal and looks to '... the intent of the artist ...' for her model of ideal listening, presuming that artists desire the undivided attention of their audiences. Lorrin may be unaware of the Ambient Music of Brian Eno or the *Musique d'ameublement* (furniture music) of Erik Satie (see Toop 2001). Nonetheless, Lorrin feels her appreciation of music is not diminished by her distraction and that occasional distraction is inevitable. There are two related perspectives here. First, Davies regrets the desensitisation of listeners as a result of increased exposure to music in its recorded form.

Second, Lorrin, perhaps representing many listeners, considers her distracted listening inevitable even while at a concert, but can see how it may be at odds with the wishes of the musician. Lorrin's account of her own listening supports Davies' opinion that most musical listening is distracted. However, Lorrin's opinion that distracted listening is not necessarily regrettable is at variance with Davies' disapproval of listening of this nature.

Temporal Manipulation

In an essay first published in 1928, Valéry provides an insightful and prescient examination of the production and reproduction of multiple copies of works of art. With regard specifically to music, and of great relevance to examination of the functions of portable music and boundary demarcation in particular, Valéry writes:

> It [music] is of all the arts the most in demand, the most involved in social existence, the closest to life, whose organic functioning it animates, accompanies, or imitates. Whether it be a matter of speaking or walking, of meditation or action, of monotony or surprise in the temporal flow of our lives, music can take hold of us, combining and transfiguring the pace and sensory values of them all. (Valéry 1964 [1928]:226)

This study's examination of portable music's functions demonstrates many examples of music's involvement in social existence, such as those observed by Valéry. For instance, aestheticisation and environmental control, examined above, are examples of ways in which portable music modifies listeners' experience of their surroundings and their interactions with people within them. Valéry's reference to music's transfiguration of the sensory values of life's experiences is particularly relevant to aestheticisation. With regard to boundary demarcation, Valéry proposes a broad mechanism by which music transfigures listeners' experiences of their surroundings, writing 'It weaves us an artificial span of time …' (1964 [1928]:226). This idea is further developed in the writing of Eisenberg, to whom this study now turns and who specifically discusses portable music, although it is important to note that Valéry was the first to expound the idea.

Eisenberg suggests the reason for listeners' use of headphones '… is the sense they give that one has escaped the city's voracity, because one is inside the music' (1988:44–45). Eisenberg's references in this sentence to both music and headphones are noteworthy in that these

•CHAPTER THREE•

are the key elements of the experience of portable music. His use of the term 'voracity' can be understood in light of his description of the city, which represents the environment from which mobile listeners attempt to remove themselves in boundary demarcation. He observes:

> ... living in the present is (contrary to vulgar opinion) nearly impossible in the modern city, which always hungers for the future and eats the past. (1988:44)

For Eisenberg, portable music allows listeners to realise the present and to overcome a multitude of competing time structures such as '... the business day, the schedules of radio and television, the neighbour's lifestyles and *their* music' (1988:44, italics in original). Eisenberg maintains that portable music allows listeners to construct a sense of personal time to negate the conflicting time structures of other people and organisations. His discussion is reminiscent of the more common idea, noted above, that portable music creates a personal space for listeners in opposition to the public space in which the mobile listener actually exists. Within their personal time, listeners can undertake their desired activities to the accompaniment of portable music. Eisenberg subsequently investigates the qualities of music that enable individual listeners to use it in the manner described above. He writes:

> A record is a sculpted block of time, repeatable at the owner's whim. That block may have been carved from another time and place (though only live recordings are carved in one piece) and so may be a document or record of its quarry. But a record of music does not exist in historical time, is not of it. A violoncello is already a time machine, taking its listener to a place outside time. The phonograph is also a time machine of this sort, but with the difference that the listener operates it himself and can take a spin as often as he pleases. (1988:46)

Musical sounds function within a framework of time as colours and shapes operate within the boundaries of a canvas to appear as an aesthetic, coherent whole. Listeners' heightened awareness of the duration and succession of musical events is the key to music's capacity to impose its own time-structures upon them. Music catches listeners up in its flow and their sense of time is governed by the succession of musical events rather than by chronometry. It is in this sense Eisenberg refers to the violoncello as a time machine. He could have referred to any source of musical sound, and recording only adds the potential for listeners to exploit this phenomenon at the time and place of their choosing.

Eisenberg's and Gumpert's ideas, reviewed earlier in the discussion of boundary demarcation, are not mutually exclusive. As noted, Gumpert understands that music demarcates a personal space around listeners while Eisenberg suggests that a listener's sense of musical time is the key. In the case of portable music, which is effectively heard only by the mobile listener concerned, there is no means by which the music can demonstrate the boundaries of the listener's personal space to bystanders. However, mobile listeners experience for themselves the sense of personal space that portable music marks out as well as the sense of musical time, and consequently feel removed from their surroundings.

Social Isolation?

Boundary demarcation involves listeners' isolation from their surroundings and, in pursuing this isolation, listeners also separate themselves from people within their surroundings. In this manner, boundary demarcation has social consequences. Some writers, for example, Adler and Negus, understand that mobile listeners can completely isolate themselves from their surroundings, eliminating all interaction with both animate and inanimate elements. By comparison, Chambers feels that any isolation mobile listeners might perceive is false and that mobile listening only confirms listeners' interactions with their surroundings. It is now appropriate to pursue these issues.

Adler observes that mobile listeners revel '... in the solitary world of a personal stereo' (1999), suggesting that mobile listeners are able to segregate themselves from their surroundings and achieve isolation. Negus similarly observes listeners' mobile isolation and also discusses the social consequences of mobile listening. He writes:

> The Walkman enables its user to take music wherever they go and exclude the external world and other human beings. It may enable Japanese commuters to cope with crowded subway trains, but the Walkman induces a sense of solipsism. It isolates individuals from the world through music ... (1992:35)

Negus continues that the Walkman allows the listener to '... shut out society ...' (1992:36) and thus explicitly rejects the possibility that mobile listening has any socially interactive component. Chambers' understanding of the mobile listening experience, however, is at odds with those of Adler and Negus. Chambers pursues the question of the effectiveness of mobile listeners' attempts to isolate themselves. While observing that mobile listening offers a '... private experience' (1994:49), Chambers also observes a degree of interaction between mobile listeners and their surroundings, writing that the Walkman:

> ... like dark glasses and iconoclastic fashion, serves to set one apart while simultaneously reaffirming individual contact to certain common, if shifting, measures ... (1994:50)

As noted above in the discussion of chosen sounds, portable music always represents the chosen listening material of the mobile listener. Making the same point, Chambers suggests that, even as portable music demarcates boundaries around listeners, it also manifests aspects of listeners' identities—portable music is the fulfilment of listeners' musical tastes. Only individual listeners can hear the portable music in question and this confirmation of the listener's preferences is therefore not evident to anyone but the listener. Nonetheless, with regard to boundary demarcation, Chambers points out that mobile listeners isolate themselves from unpleasant aspects of their surroundings even as they draw enjoyable aspects even closer, choosing to hear their preferred music transmitted intimately to them by their headphones. In this manner, mobile listening, rather than completely isolating the listener, only confirms their relations with certain chosen aspects of their surroundings. Nonetheless, Chambers acknowledges listeners' feelings, as noted above, that they are in another place, dimension or world while listening to music. He refers to listeners' '... diasporic identity ...' (1994:50), a term that implies listeners are 'dispersed' from their rightful location. Thus Chambers asserts that, while listeners are ultimately 'where they are' and inhabiting physical space, listening to music promotes a sense of 'removal' from the surroundings.

Judith Williamson's perspective varies from those reviewed to this point. She maintains a critical attitude in her discussion of mobile listening, particularly regarding annoying leakage of sound from headphones. In an observation that pertains to boundary demarcation, Williamson reasons:

> The argument that the walkman protects the *public* from hearing one person's sounds, is back-to-front: it is the walk-person who is protected from

the outside world, for whether or not their music is audible they are shut off as if in a spell. (1988:209, italics in original)

Williamson understands that some mobile listeners perceive their listening as a polite attempt not to subject others to their chosen music. Headphones contain the listener's music such that only they can hear it, although, given Williamson's complaints about leakage, this is not always successful. Williamson's understanding is unique in the discourse although it is supported by one of this study's interview subjects. In her interview, Ellen related her opinion of mobile listening that is audible to people in the vicinity:

> I find it annoying when other people are listening to Walkman on the bus because they sometimes have the volume up so loud and then it's distracting for others. I try to keep it fairly quiet and hope that I'm not disturbing anyone around. (2001)

Ellen's testimony indicates that some mobile listeners consider portable music a means by which they can satisfy their desire to listen without disturbing others. This is the reverse of the situation typically envisaged in the discussion of boundary demarcation, where listeners desire to use their music to eliminate the distractions otherwise imposed on them by their surroundings.

Williamson subsequently develops her argument and presents her understanding of mobile listening with reference to the specific social and political environment she observes:

> The walkman is a vivid symbol of our time. It provides a concrete image of alienation, suggesting an implicit hostility to, and isolation from, the environment in which it is worn. Yet it also embodies the underlying values of precisely the society which produces the alienation—those principles which are the lynch pin of Thatcherite Britain: individualism, privatization and "choice". The walkman is primarily a way of escaping from a *shared* experience or environment. It produces a privatized sound, in the public domain; a weapon of the individual against the communal. (1988:209–210, italics in original)

This is the typical view of mobile listening and, in the terminology of this study, of boundary demarcation. Listeners want to remove themselves from their environments and their portable music enables them to feel as if they have done so. This is a clear contrast with the idea that listening in public might be prompted in the first place by listeners' desire to listen and in the second place by listeners' concern that people in their vicinity should not be annoyed by sound leakage. In an account of mobile listening that is relevant to much of Williamson's writing, in his interview Joshua referred to the private nature of listening to portable music in a public space:

> It's just cool that if you're into particular types of music you can just have them on in your own little space and hopefully not disturb people around you because people on the bus don't want to be disturbed. So I think that's part of the appeal of having a Walkman, that it's a personal thing. (2001)

In this passage, Joshua supports both of Williamson's assertions. He clearly feels that mobile listening is a means by which he can enjoy his chosen music without disturbing people in his vicinity. Joshua also feels that listening to his portable music facilitates his 'own little space', and thus excludes people around him from his own experience. Although Chambers, as noted, disputes the solitary nature of this experience, the mobile listener's understanding that their experience of portable music is a solitary one is at the heart of portable music's capacity to demarcate a boundary for them. Following Joshua's feedback, listeners' enjoyment of the solitary nature of their listening does not preclude their consideration of people around them as they recognise that the leakage of portable music can be annoying.

In a further development, Bull criticises the use of a private/public duality model to discuss the experience of mobile listening. He suggests that the experience requires new thinking and terminology in order for it to be adequately examined, observing that the Walkman permits:

> ... a reorganization of public and private realms of experience, where what is traditionally conceived of as "private" experience is brought out into public realms in the act of individualized listening. (2001:210–211)

Bull ultimately finds the terms 'public' and 'private' inadequate to describe the sites of the portable music experience and suggests an alternative, writing '... urban experience becomes, in a significant manner, technological experience' (2001:211). Bull understands that the distinction between public and private fails in the face of technology that enables people in public spaces to engage in what was previously understood to be private behaviour. The concept of technological experience eliminates these problems; however, it remains inadequate in the description of the experience of portable music. As noted previously during the course of this study, Bull does not engage with the musical aspects of the experience of mobile listening, and the concept of 'technological' experience, while it overcomes the problems associated with the obsolescence of 'public' and 'private' in the face of new technology, still fails to address relevant musical issues. There are elements of the experience of portable music that can only be understood in terms of musical experience.

Studies by four scholars inform discussion of the mobile listener's experience of boundary demarcation. To begin with, Lind and Chow observe mobile listening behaviour related to boundary demarcation, although they do not examine it in any depth. In her study, Lind observes that 'it [the Walkman] allows you to create private space' (1989:59) whereas Chow describes the Walkman as '... the hiding place for the music-operator' (1999). Bull also discusses a related strategy of mobile listening, adapted in this study in order to focus on portable music and consequently to define boundary demarcation. He presents an analogy between listening and reading that, in the mould of that drawn above between film and aestheticisation, enables boundary demarcation to be easily understood. He observes:

> ... urban dwellers are reacting to the lack of personal space both bodily and visually. Personal stereos thus become a kind of mobile book or newspaper permitting users to attend to something else. In their absorption they can partially pretend that they are not really there. (2000:186)

It has been noted that portable music's capacity to overcome ambient noises contributes to the isolation it affords listeners from their environments. Bull's analysis highlights another facet of boundary demarcation, in that portable music also engages listeners' attention so they are distracted from their surroundings, which consequently no longer impinge upon them. Chen makes the same point and draws a comparison between mobile listening and reading. She writes:

> Even though reading is an individualistic act, reading does not prevent intrusion from others. Walkman listening, by impairing the hearing of outside sources of sound, and by enveloping one in a surrounding filled with rhythm, melody, images, and emotions, can more completely cut the listener off from the external environment. (1993:93)

Chen's comparison suggests that portable music presents listeners with a smorgasbord of musical delights (rhythm, melody) as well as the meanings they hold for listeners (images, emotions) which tempt their attention away from what is happening within their surroundings. Chen's comparison suggests that listening to portable music is even more effective than reading a book for eliminating contact with the surroundings. In addition to engaging listeners' attention, portable music also eliminates ambient noises. This double action is a highly effective means by which listeners can use portable music to control their interactions with their surroundings. Chen subsequently adapts the concept of narcissism in order to present her understanding of the mobile listening experience. Informed by her reading of Freud, Chen defines narcissism as '... a state of self-absorption in which the individual withdraws from the external environment, disengages from social activities, and is indifferent to others' (1993:95). The listener's withdrawal from the external environment corresponds to boundary demarcation and Chen relates her concept of narcissism to the experience of portable music as follows:

> The Walkman enables individual listeners to enjoy in private the visceral sensations called up by the music. As one indulges in experiencing private sensations, one is fully wrapped up in one's own world. (1993:95)

Chen suggests it is music's ability to generate visceral sensations in listeners that enables it to remove listeners from their surroundings. Chen does not explain the origins of music's ability to generate visceral sensations, but her observation seems to correspond to music's capacity to engage listeners' attention and consequently remove it from their surroundings. Further, Chen's observation that listeners are wrapped up in their own worlds corresponds with the feelings, cited above, of mobile listeners such as Darryl, Ellen, and Scott. These listeners felt as if they were in 'their own world' or in 'a different place' while listening to portable music. By the various means that writers and listeners understand it to act, portable music defines boundaries around listeners, setting them apart from environments they otherwise find unpleasant.

Function Six: Interpersonal Mediation

Interpersonal mediation, in which the act of listening to portable music modifies interactions between listeners and bystanders, comprises three modes. In the first, portable music overwhelms external noises and renders mobile listeners unable to hear bystanders' attempts to gain their attention. Although listeners might normally choose to interact, they remain unaware of the opportunity to do so and their personal interactions are modified as a result. In the second mode, mobile listeners' attention is directed toward their portable music and not toward their surroundings or toward bystanders. Thus distracted, listeners are unaware of opportunities to interact with others and their personal interactions are modified once again. In the third mode, the Walkman or iPod apparatus itself modifies mobile listeners' personal interactions. The visible presence of the apparatus (especially the headphones) on a listener's person tells bystanders that listeners might not hear them or notice their attempts to interact with them. Bystanders consequently choose not to interact with mobile listeners since attempts to initiate interaction are unnecessarily difficult and potentially futile. For bystanders, portable music plays no direct role in the modification of social interaction because, apart from leakage, they cannot hear it. Thus, interpersonal mediation's third mode cannot be considered a function of portable music, but it is examined here because it often occurs simultaneously with the first and second modes.

An important point arises when the early responses to the Walkman and this study's interviews are reviewed. The Walkman's effect on personal interactions was often people's first impression of the device and its reception was often cool as a result. This feeling has subsided in the years since the Walkman's introduction and the iPod received no negative press of this nature, but such a response features in Morita's[5] account of some very early mobile listening, occurring when he tested a prototype Walkman at home. Morita states:

> I rushed home with the first Walkman and was trying it out with different music when I noticed that my experiment was annoying my wife, who felt shut out. All right, I decided, we need to make provision for two sets of headphones. The next week the production staff had produced another model with two headphone jacks. (1986:80)

This is probably the first instance of the modification of personal interactions by portable music and thus of interpersonal mediation, although it is impossible to determine if Morita's anecdote is an example of the first or second mode. Morita's wife's displeasure is also the first recorded example of a negative response to another person's mobile listening and is sufficiently forceful that Morita instigated modifications to the original Walkman design. As indicated above, similar negative responses are documented in other literature and in this study's fieldwork results. From the literature, Lind responds to Morita's account of the development of the Walkman and also notes the immediate negative response to the Walkman's effect on personal interaction. She observes:

> ... the potential interaction of personal stereo use and interpersonal communication was considered from the very beginning of Walkman product development. Further, the potential impact was deemed to be something which should be remedied, hence, the addition of extra jacks and the "hot line" feature [which reduces playback volume and allows sharing listeners to converse without removing their headphones]. Because these attempts were made to neutralize this situation, we may assume that the personal stereo was at first considered to have a potentially negative influence on interpersonal communication. (1989:3)

Lind's study also provides fieldwork evidence of negative responses from bystanders toward Walkman listeners. Lind discovers that '... there is a powerful norm of not initiating conversation with a personal stereo user' (1989:99). Bystanders consider interpersonal communication with a mobile listener 'too hard' (1989:80), or mobile listeners themselves 'too rude' (1989:80) or 'too loud' (1989:80). Descriptions such as 'too loud' and 'too rude' exemplify negative responses to mobile listening and the associated modification of bystanders' interactions with mobile listeners.

From this study's interviews, Campbell would rather interact socially with fellow bus passengers than listen to portable music. He felt that excluding fellow commuters is a regrettable consequence of mobile listening:

> I definitely use it [the Walkman] on buses but I'm always looking for an opportunity to talk to somebody. Very rarely do I use the Walkman when I'm around conversable [sic] people. I live in the hills so it's a very communal bus; it's always a pleasure to meet somebody. (2001)

Similarly, in his interview and in a more explicit example than Campbell's of a negative response to mobile listening, Darryl regrets mobile listening that diminishes personal interaction. He stated:

> Well, so many people have them [Walkmans or iPods] on the train. I think it actually saves people actually communicating. It's a sad thing in one way that people don't communicate as much. (2001)

Darryl thinks it is sad that commuters listen to portable music rather than communicating with their fellows. He feels that engaging his peers in conversation would be preferable to shutting them out as a consequence of his mobile listening.

Another interview response, from Daniel, is an amusing example of interpersonal mediation and one to which his fellow passengers would probably respond negatively:

> It's funny, you know. If you're on the train and sitting next to some people and listening to your Walkman, if the tape runs out and you rewind it you can hear what they are saying. I remember, that happened and these two people were having this really intimate conversation while I was within earshot, because they thought I was listening to the Walkman and couldn't hear. You could have a lot of fun that way, although I didn't. (2001)

In an example of the third mode of interpersonal mediation, Daniel's interaction with his fellow passengers is modified because of his apparent listening. The visible presence of Daniel's Walkman headphones gives his fellow passengers the (mistaken) impression his attention is directed toward his music and that he cannot hear their conversation.

In the case of interpersonal mediation, discussion of the social consequences of mobile listening assumes great importance because social interaction, its avoidance and modification by listeners, is at the heart of this function. Interactions between listeners and bystanders are not social in the sense that they concern companionship, cooperation or mutually enjoyable interaction. Rather, interactions between mobile listeners and bystanders are social only because they involve more than one person. The key point arising from the review of relevant sources is that, even though some mobile listeners might intend to eliminate interactions with bystanders as they listen, they cannot entirely do so. In modified form, interactions still take place between mobile listeners and people in their vicinity. Gumpert observes:

> The earphones establish an acoustical territory which is not to be entered without permission and which restricts interaction with outsiders. The wall of sound is silent, but communicates quite clearly. The presence of a Walkman renders the outsider invisible – a strange and unsettling feeling. It is equally strange to witness a person gyrating and foot-tapping to an imperceptible beat. The suspicion of a possible mental disturbance vanishes with the sight of an earphone, and the alien walks and jogs to the beat of a different tape. (1987:91)

This statement captures Gumpert's understanding of the bystander's perspective, the person who is deterred in their attempts to interact with their mobile listening acquaintances. Gumpert's observations correspond to the third mode of interpersonal mediation. He notes that, apart from the Walkman or iPod apparatus, bystanders might also observe mobile listeners as they gyrate or display other evidence of their listening. This is an extension of the third mode of interpersonal mediation, in which listeners' physical responses to their portable music discourages bystanders from attempting to interact with them. Stephen, one of this study's interviewees, relates an instance from his experience that corresponds to Gumpert's observation:

> Some people get on the bus with [portable] music and everyone on the bus can hear it. They've only got little earphones in their ears and I hate to imagine what on earth it's doing to their ears. You can actually see when they get on the bus that they're very, very energised. So the music's having a big effect on their brain, that's for sure. (2001)

Listeners' responses to portable music might not always be as apparent as in Stephen's example, but mobile listening is sometimes obvious to bystanders and tends to set listeners apart from their surroundings. Portable music, however, cannot entirely preclude the potential for interaction and Stephen's consideration of mobile listeners whom he observes on the bus is an example of possible interaction between listeners and bystanders. As noted, this is not social interaction in the sense of mutual enjoyment, but is based around an individual's mobile listening and observers' responses to it.

Chambers' writing, reviewed above as it relates to boundary demarcation, is also relevant here. As noted, he argues that mobile listening cannot entirely eliminate listeners' interactions with their surroundings and writes 'In the manifest refusal of sociability the Walkman nevertheless reaffirms participation in a shared environment' (1994:50). Morita's anecdotes, the fieldwork accounts of mobile listening gained through interviews, and Gumpert's ideas, presented above, all support Chambers' assertion that mobile listening modifies, but does not eliminate, listeners' social interactions. Mobile listeners remain aware of modified social interactions that take place as they listen. For example, Morita is aware of his wife's displeasure as he tests his prototype, to the extent he is motivated to order modifications to it. Morita's listening does not dismiss his wife from his thoughts. Rather, Morita's loving relationship with his wife and the consideration he gives to her opinions are confirmed. In another example, Darryl, despite the contribution of his own mobile listening to the silence, finds the lack of communication between people on public transport sad, thus affirming his empathy with fellow passengers.

In a published interview with Stephen Fenichell, Welsh rock-and-roll musician Dave Edmunds expresses an etiquette of mobile listening that differs slightly from those reproduced above, although it also confirms Edmunds' presence in a shared environment. Edmunds states:

> ... I do find the personal stereo terrifically handy, because I get sent a lot of cassettes by budding songwriters and bands, and usually they're not very good. So it's quite nice to be able to play all this stuff without making such a nuisance of myself around other people. The unit is also invaluable on the tour bus because you're practically living together, you and the band, and it's important not to get on anyone's nerves. With these things, people can listen to whatever they want. (Fenichell 1983:140–141)

Edmunds considers his mobile listening to be an act of courtesy. His headphones allow him to listen, while not obliging people in his vicinity to also hear his music. Other means of playing his tapes would involve a greater degree of 'leakage' of the sound so that fellow inhabitants of the bus would hear it and possibly be annoyed by it. Edmunds' account supports Chambers' assertion that mobile listeners' surroundings remain tenaciously present despite the distractions of their portable music. Edmunds' band mates are foremost in his thoughts as he listens, as evidenced by his conscious efforts to maintain good relations with them.

Hosokawa presents a theory that informs discussion of the bystander's perspective as well as of the social interactions inherent to interpersonal mediation. As discussed in Chapter One, he discusses mobile listeners as secret-holders (only they know what they are listening to) and bystanders as secret-beholders (they see the mobile listener is listening to something but cannot know what it is). Hosokawa develops this idea, explaining a possible basis of ill will that bystanders might direct toward mobile listeners. Understanding that 'The secret-holder always has an advantage over the secret-beholder ...' (1984:177), Hosokawa suggests:

> The superiority felt by the holder to the beholder is far from the casual satisfaction of acquiring something fashionable, but relates to receiving the visa for the secret garden of the walkman in which people communicate with

one another through the form—not the content—of the secret. (1984:177–178)

Hosokawa refers to the sounds of portable music as the 'content' of a secret. As discussed above, apart from the possibility of slight leakage, bystanders cannot respond to portable music because they cannot hear it. Bystanders can only respond to the appearance of the Walkman or iPod and their understanding of what that appearance entails; namely, to what Hosokawa terms the 'form' of the secret. Hosokawa is unique in the literature in drawing a distinction between the physical appearance of the Walkman or iPod to bystanders on the one hand and portable music on the other. This distinction is reflected in this study's approach to the examination of interpersonal mediation's three modes. As noted, the first and second modes are considered functions of portable music while the third mode relates to the visible presence of the Walkman or iPod itself.

In a discussion pertaining to interpersonal mediation's third mode, Hosokawa further develops his idea of secret theatre. He writes:

> ... with the appearance of this novel gadget [the Walkman or iPod], all passers-by are inevitably involved in the ... theatre, as either actors (holders) or spectators (beholders) ... (1984:179)

Hosokawa asserts that bystanders must be involved in mobile listening, even if it is the listener's goal to make themselves unavailable for personal interaction with them. The visible presence of the Walkman or iPod alerts bystanders to mobile listeners and they are intrigued. Bystanders do not interact with mobile listeners in the sense of engaging in conversation, but the combined acts of listening on the one hand and curiously observing on the other hand must be considered a form of interaction. Hosokawa aptly compares this interaction to '... the theatrical process ...' (1984:178) in which listeners are actors and observers are members of the audience.

Adorno presents an account of music listening using early headphones which relates closely to Hosokawa's discussion. He writes:

> In Nice, on the other side far away from the big hotels, there is a locale where, with considerable effort, one extracts some publicity from the gramophone whose private character is conserved in French fashion. There, along the walls in sealed glass cases, one finds twenty gramophones lined up one next to another, each of which doggedly services one record. The

gramophones are operated automatically by inserting a token. In order to hear something, one has to put on a pair of headphones: those who don't pay hear nothing. (1990a:52–53)

Adorno observes that the audience for these gramophones ('... petit bourgeois girls, most of them underage' [1990a:53]) are also the object of passers-by's attention. The girls '... wait for someone to approach them' (1990a:53). Here Adorno observes a paradox. Because of the headphones, only the petit bourgeois girls can hear their chosen music as it is reproduced by the gramophone. The privacy of their listening attracts attention and the girls, knowing this, take advantage of it and wait to be approached. Thus, their private listening is effectively a public ploy for attention. In Adorno's words, the private character of gramophone listening is conserved while listeners simultaneously extract some publicity from their listening. Likewise, adapting Hosokawa's words, all passers-by are inevitably involved in the gramophone-theatre.

In her study of the Walkman, Lind proposes three effects of mobile listening that relate to interpersonal mediation. Lind's discussion captures the perspective of bystanders for whom interaction with mobile listeners is modified, if not entirely eliminated. She observes:

> ... because any existing sound environment can be substituted with whatever the user prefers, others who may be physically close to the user do not experience the same environment. This inability to share a common environment may act to separate personal stereo users from others. (1989:8)

In her observation that portable music replaces any existing sound environment, Lind's comments are pertinent to the first mode of interpersonal mediation. Lind suggests that mobile listening disrupts listeners' presence in the aural environment they would normally share with people in their vicinity. Listeners are 'separated' from bystanders (with whom they could otherwise easily interact by speaking) because they do not share an audible environment with them.

To briefly digress, in his reference to the breakdown in the common environment that the Walkman or iPod precipitates, Rainer Schönhammer's understanding of the impression that mobile listeners make on passers-by relates to Lind's assertion. He presents his understanding of the reasons for the generally negative nature of this impression, writing:

> We see the earphone user as living in a private acoustic world which we are unable to share. This seems to interrupt a form of contact between "normal" people in a shared situation, even if there is no explicit communication at all. People with earphones seem to violate an unwritten law of interpersonal reciprocity: the certainty of common sensual presence in shared situations. (1989:130)

First, Schönhammer understands mobile listening as deviant; it interrupts contact between 'normal' people. This is another instance of a negative response to changes portable music makes to listeners' personal interactions. Second, Schönhammer explicitly outlines an idea only hinted at by Lind. This is the concept that people within a given vicinity normally share, in the words of Schönhammer, '... a common sensual presence ...' (1989:130), or that, in the words of Lind, they experience the same environment (1989:8). Schönhammer's discussion combines elements of the first and third modes of interpersonal mediation. Mobile listeners' existence in a private acoustic world is an instance of interpersonal mediation's first mode. However, more than a simple inability to hear, Schönhammer suggests mobile listeners' obvious removal from the common aural environment or soundscape deters bystanders' attempts to interact. Schönhammer refers to bystanders 'seeing' the earphone user and drawing conclusions regarding their presence in the shared soundscape and thus about the mobile listener's availability for interaction. This is the third mode of interpersonal mediation. Lind's and Schönhammer's observations illustrate that, in reality, several modes of interpersonal mediation occur simultaneously.

Returning to Lind's thoughts, she suggests that '... users may be perceived as seeking "private space", thereby potentially constraining interpersonal communication' (1989:1). Lind's reference to listeners' private space clearly links her observations to the second mode of interpersonal mediation. Although she examines the '... effects ...' (1989:1) of the personal stereo, Lind's observations bring the role of portable music into sharp relief. She writes 'Because the listening experience is so private, others are excluded from listening—in effect, isolating the listener' (1989:8). In its focus on the listening experience, Lind's approach implicitly acknowledges that portable music plays the key role in the constraint of interpersonal communication that she observes. After all, in order to be distracted from their surroundings, as is the case in interpersonal mediation's second mode, listeners need something with which to be distracted and portable music provides substantially more scope for distraction than the Walkman or iPod apparatus by itself. Third, and relevant to the third mode of interpersonal mediation, Lind turns to generally prevalent attitudes regarding the Walkman and iPod. She writes:

> ... an individual is expected to *either* use a personal stereo *or* interact with others. The attitude seems to be that these activities are mutually exclusive. (1989:101, italics in original)

Lind's discussion encapsulates interpersonal mediation from the bystander's perspective. One implication of the expectation she discusses is that people cannot satisfactorily interact with their fellows while listening to portable music, if interaction can even be initiated in the first place. As noted, the consequence of this expectation is that people are less likely to attempt to engage mobile listeners in interaction.

Finally, Walkman users' modified interactions with other people is the source of satire in *The Onion* (Dickers 1999).[6] Describing the Walkman as a '... portable populace-pacification device ...' (1999:130), *The Onion* suggests it '... transports its user to a warm, self-contained aural environment, freeing him from social interaction with others' (1999:130). Then, ascribing the observations it publishes to fictional Sony spokesperson David Gelfand, *The Onion* alleges the Walkman is '... superior to other music-playing devices in that it not only plays music but also blocks out one's awareness of the rest of the world' (1999:130). The best consequence of this isolation is that:

> ... any sound below 60 decibels—including the voices of nagging authority figures, co-workers, intrusive bus patrons or loved ones—is eliminated, along with the need to respond. (1999:130)

Sony allegedly predicts:

> When each and every American consumer is outfitted with this small metal box and the accompanying length of cord and two sponge-like ear-mounted speakers, all forms of discontent will cease to exist. (1999:130)

It was noted above that the consequences for personal interactions of mobile listening have generated many responses in the literature. Although *The Onion* exaggerates the consequences of Walkman use for the sake of satire, it is significant that the isolating qualities of the experience of portable music are sufficiently apparent and ubiquitous that they are subject to mockery.

Chen's writing is of particular interest here because it corresponds closely to this study's analysis. She discusses the individual experience of mobile listening, and presents examples that correspond to interpersonal mediation's first and second modes. Related to the first mode, she examines mobile listening among college students and observes '... the impairment of hearing [as a result of listening to portable music] makes intrusion from others difficult' (1993:109). Also, related to interpersonal mediation's second mode, she writes:

> The use of the Walkman creates social segregation, with the enveloping musical environment decreasing the likelihood of social interaction. The anti-social tendency allows an individual to use the device to create an invisible private world out of the existing social environment, segregating herself from others. (1993:108)

Chen notes that the segregation she observes occurs as a result of '... the enveloping musical environment ...' (1993:108), and thus indicates the role of portable music in the modification of listeners' personal interactions. She suggests that mobile listeners are immersed in their own music-related thoughts and consequently distracted from their surroundings. This is another example of interpersonal mediation's second mode.

Interpersonal mediation can be a result of mobile listeners' intentional efforts to render themselves unavailable for personal interaction. In an instance of intentional interpersonal mediation, Chen presents an example from her fieldwork. Her informant, Shane, relates:

> While sitting outside, I spied somebody coming toward me. I can't STAND this person because she talks my leg off about trivial matters that I care nothing about. Quick! On with the Walkman and break open my note pad. The Dragon Lady passes. (1993)

Interpersonal mediation can also be unintentional. As noted in the discussion of chosen sounds, mobile listeners often listen for the sake of the music. In such instances portable music blocks out ambient noise and engages listeners' attention. Modification of the listener's personal interactions by the first and second modes of interpersonal mediation results, although listening and not interpersonal mediation is the mobile listener's primary intent.

The perspective of bystanders is discussed above. Lind and Bull discuss the other important perspective in interpersonal mediation's third mode, that of the mobile listener. First, in her study of the Walkman, Lind examines fourteen reasons for personal stereo use and ranks them according to the frequency of their occurrence within her study group. 'It's a way to let others know you don't want to be disturbed' (1989:59) and 'It provides distraction in an uncomfortable social setting' (1989:59) correspond to interpersonal mediation and are respectively the tenth and thirteenth most frequent of those Lind examines. These reasons capture the motivations of mobile listeners who listen to avoid interactions with other people. Second, Bull observes that users '... sometimes even pretend to listen' (2000:190) in order to avoid unwanted personal interaction. This further demonstrates portable music's noninvolvement in interpersonal mediation's third mode. Bystanders make judgments on mobile listeners' availability for interaction on the basis of the presence of the Walkman or iPod apparatus. Aware of this, mobile listeners may choose to wear their Walkmans or iPods when they want to avoid interacting with others. As Bull observes, mobile listeners:

> ... feel that other people do not trouble them so much as they are harder to approach. Users often describe feeling more confident in public wearing their personal stereos. Personal stereos are visual "do not disturb" signs. They are also an efficient tool for controlling the manner and nature of contact with others. (2000:189)

Bull's examination of strategies of Walkman use is criticised in this study because it does not acknowledge the role of portable music. However, as it relates to the third mode of interpersonal mediation, Bull's focus on the Walkman apparatus rather than on portable music is entirely appropriate.

Adorno also offers insights which relate to the mobile listener's perspective of interpersonal mediation. His insights, particularly into the role of music, are at odds with those examined to this point. The sources examined above (Bull, Chen, and Lind) suggest that listening to portable music modifies personal interactions between mobile listeners and others. By contrast, Adorno asserts that communication between people is diminishing anyway and that music:

> ... seems to complement the reduction of people to silence, the dying out of speech as expression, the inability to communicate at all. It inhibits the pockets of silence that develop between people molded by anxiety, work and undemanding docility. Everywhere it takes over, unnoticed, the deadly sad role that fell to it in the time and the specific situation of the silent films. It is

perceived purely as background. If nobody can any longer speak, then certainly nobody can any longer listen. (1978:271)

Adorno suggests that work, anxiety, and docility result in the decreased ability of people to speak or communicate and that background music distracts people from the depressing silence that results. As noted, in this study the functions of portable music are examined and portable music is understood to play a causal role in listener's experiences. The first and second modes of interpersonal mediation, in which portable music blocks out bystanders' otherwise audible attempts to interact with mobile listeners and distracts listeners from such attempts respectively, exemplify this perspective. In light of Adorno's reasoning, the role of portable music in interpersonal mediation could be understood as a complement to or distraction from mobile listeners' inability to communicate in the first place rather than the cause of their diminished communication.

Having reviewed published sources pertaining to the mobile listener's experience of interpersonal mediation, it is appropriate to turn to this study's fieldwork results. The personal accounts included here provide insight into subtleties and nuances of the experience that are not represented in the literature. First, in her interview, Aliese related that she initially suspected shop assistants only greeted her out of ulterior commercial motives. This suspicion motivated Aliese to continue her mobile listening after entering shops and she was subsequently surprised to find shop assistants regarded her consequent nonavailability for personal interaction as rude and antisocial. Aliese persisted with her listening nonetheless, consciously deciding not to pay shop assistants the courtesy of removing her headphones and thus making herself available for interaction. She related:

> I couldn't be bothered [taking my headphones off] and I thought, "I'm just going to hop in this shop for five seconds and look at this book and then hop back out again so what's the point?". I really thought of it as a courtesy thing. I thought, "I can't be bothered to give these people the courtesy of taking my Walkman off right now". Wearing my Walkman, it's like I'm saying, "I'm just here shopping". Shop assistants come up to you and they say "How are you today?" and if you're wearing your Walkman they can't do that and then they wonder why you're not talking to them. This girl came up and said "Hello" and I didn't say anything and then I turned around and said "Sorry, I'm wearing my Walkman" and then she said "Well, aren't we antisocial?" and I thought that was really funny. That's why the Walkman is good; you cut out that bit where they make contact with you. (2001)

Aliese regards her headphones as an outward manifestation of her intent not to interact with others and, by not removing them, makes a conscious decision to be discourteous and antisocial in the eyes of people with whom she might otherwise interact. She is aware that her mobile listening can be viewed negatively by bystanders. It is noteworthy that Aliese does not mention her desire to listen to music but thinks her Walkman is good because it cuts '… out that bit where they [shopkeepers] make contact with you' (2001). If portable music is understood to be the mobile listener's chosen listening material, as noted in the examination of chosen sounds, then portable music's other functions, including interpersonal mediation, might be regarded almost as side effects of the mobile listener's decision to hear their chosen music. Aliese's account of her mobile listening supports the understanding that at times interpersonal mediation, rather than the desire to listen to portable music, is mobile listeners' primary motivation.

Aliese's listening practices go further than avoiding conversation or interaction with shop assistants to behaviour verging on queue jumping. She related:

> … when I'm wearing my Walkman I'm a lot more aggressive getting in lines as well. I'll wait for an old lady who's sort of a bit dazed and then stand in front of her or something. Placebo[7] encourages me to do that. It's easier to see people as enemies if you can't really hear what they're saying or what they're doing or whatever. And also, you can't hear if you're making a big noise coming up to people so you think of yourself as the stealth machine, you know, "just going to stealthily move in front of this old lady". (2001)

It is noted above that Aliese continues listening to portable music after entering shops to avoid interacting with shop assistants while she browses. The second extract from her interview suggests Aliese's experience of portable music changes her attitude toward people in her vicinity even more markedly than noted in that instance. In addition to reducing the probability that Aliese will engage in social interaction with them, Aliese's mobile listening disengages her from people around her to the extent that she consciously views them as obstacles or adversaries, even enemies. Furthermore, Aliese is aware, even at the time it occurs, that her behaviour changes as a result of her listening. By contrast, Daniel is unaware of interpersonal mediation while he listens to portable music:

• CHAPTER THREE •

> I constantly had the Walkman on and the earphones in. I remember when I was 15 at school, the whole schoolyard courtship thing, and my girlfriend at the time complained. She was annoyed because she reckoned that she couldn't get my attention in the school corridor. I don't know. Apparently I was always walking along with my head down and earplugs in my ears. My friends still pay me out about it. (2001)

Daniel only became aware that his listening was excluding people who wanted to interact with him when they told him about it after the fact. Further, even someone as close to Daniel as his girlfriend of the time found him difficult to approach because his portable music distracted him so much. In addition to their interactions with strangers, portable music also influences mobile listeners' interactions with people with whom they share close relationships. This was also demonstrated by Morita's wife's response to his early Walkman testing.

Scott's mobile listening is of interest because he is aware of bystanders' points of view. First he recounted his own understanding of his listening experiences on buses:

> I pretty much ignore them [fellow bus commuters] you know. I pretty much just listen to the music and get into the music. I'm not really worried about what everyone else is doing. (2001)

Scott's listening is an example of the second mode of interpersonal mediation. Regarding bystanders whom he ignores, Scott states:

> I think they pretty much ignore me. They see I've got a Walkman on and they don't talk to you, they just sort of sit next to you. (2001)

In Scott's eyes (but in this study's terminology) the third mode of interpersonal mediation is at play. Similar to the reaction noted by Aliese, Scott is aware of the effect his mobile listening is having on his interactions with people around him.

Steven's mobile listening is an example of interpersonal mediation's first mode; he cannot hear attempts to get his attention. Like Scott and Aliese, he is aware of the effect his obvious listening has on his neighbours. He recalls:

> The main bus route that I used went all the way into the icky centre of Salisbury[8] (though I only rode it to the edge), so there were many undesirables on the bus. Apart from the obvious shielding effect of not being able to hear their drunken/psychotic ramblings, it also gave an extra layer of protection. Perhaps you are less of a target because the wires dangling from

your ears indicate that your attention will be slightly more difficult to secure. (2001)

In addition to the first mode, Steven's listening also involves elements of the third mode of interpersonal mediation; he understands that the wires associated with his headphones make him less of a 'target' for the attentions of people with whom he would rather not converse.

Aaron's mobile listening also takes place on public transport although Aaron does not necessarily enjoy the interpersonal mediation that results. He related:

> It [mobile listening] does change the experience [of being on a bus]. It blocks you out from everything. If people see you with earphones on you're almost not there. They realise that you can't hear them and you're switched off to anything, any sort of interaction. In that way I don't really like it because it sort of shuts you off from the world. I do it when it's necessary, when there's something I have to listen to, as in preparing or analysing a piece [of music] but apart from that I don't tend to listen to much on the bus any more. I realise a lot of people do listen on the bus, there's a whole group of people and they're all facing forwards and some people want to shut themselves off. It's something to do with living in a city sort of society where you're dealing with lots of people all the time. So I don't like that. I guess that's why I stopped doing it. I saw lots of people with headphones and it just shuts you off from a possible experience that you might have on a bus. (2001)

Aaron's listening is an example of the second mode of interpersonal mediation. His concentration on the music he is preparing or analysing distracts him from his fellow passengers. Further, Aaron is aware of the effect of his mobile listening and observes the third mode of interpersonal mediation in action. He notes that passengers realise he can't hear them and that he is switched off to any sort of interaction. Similar to the comments of Darryl and Campbell, noted above, Aaron regrets the reduction in personal interaction brought about by his mobile listening. When he does not absolutely need to listen, Aaron would prefer to maximise his chances of experiencing some sort of personal interaction by leaving his headphones off.

Varying personal experiences of interpersonal mediation are observed in the personal accounts of mobile listening cited in this chapter. Some listeners intentionally avoid personal interactions, well aware of the effect their visible headphones have on bystanders. Other listeners are primarily focussed on their music and only become aware that their personal interactions have been disrupted when their friends complain. Another group of listeners need to listen on occasion, but prefer not to because they are aware of the deleterious effects of their listening on interactions with others. It is noteworthy that many listeners have a negative view of the disruption to personal interactions brought about by their listening. Bystanders for whom interaction with listeners is disrupted also respond negatively to the experience. It is also noteworthy that the broad range of experiences reviewed in this chapter all relate directly to portable music. Even bystanders who cannot hear a mobile listener's portable music are aware of the effect it has on listeners and understand their modified interactions with the listener in those terms.

Notes

[1] Landmark and common rendezvous point in Adelaide, Australia.
[2] "Discman" is Sony's brand name for portable stereos that play music from compact discs.
[3] 3D-CAD means three-dimensional computer aided design.
[4] This anonymous author uses 'Walkmen' as the plural of 'Walkman'. As the observant reader will have noted, in this study, 'Walkmans' is the preferred plural of 'Walkman'.
[5] Akio Morita and Masaru Ibuka were co-founders of the Sony corporation, manufacturers of the original Walkman.
[6] *The Onion* is an internet-based satirical newspaper. The extracts cited in this study are sourced from a hard-copy compilation of *Onion* highlights. (see Dickers 1999)
[7] Placebo are a UK rock band.
[8] Salisbury is a satellite city of Adelaide, Australia, the city in which this study was based.

• CHAPTER FOUR •

Company, Aural Mnemonic, Mood Management, Time Management, and Activation

In the five functions of portable music examined in this chapter, mobile listeners use their music to manage aspects of their own experience. In company, listeners use portable music as a substitute companion and to alleviate loneliness. In aural mnemonic, listeners use portable music to aid their recollection of enjoyable memories. In mood management, mobile listeners use portable music to improve undesirable moods or to sustain good moods. In time management, people listen to portable music instead of resigning themselves to complete lack of activity or instead of undertaking activities they consider boring or monotonous. Finally, in activation, mobile listeners move to the rhythm of the music and often undertake more strenuous physical activity as a result. In each of these functions, portable music's convenience allows listeners to enhance their daily routines at the times and places of their choosing.

Function Seven: Company

In company, mobile listeners use portable music to assuage loneliness. To these listeners, portable music conveys the presence of the musicians who created it and thus acts as a substitute companion. Adorno features significantly in the examination of company, and his earliest relevant discussion is presented in *Philosophy of Modern Music* (1973). This source was originally published in German in 1948, and it is noteworthy that Adorno first observed one of the subtler consequences of recording music so long ago. Adorno suggests that solitary listeners associate the sound of recorded music with the presence of performers who would play that music in live performance, and thus experience a form of pseudo-interaction as they listen. Leppert notes this aspect of Adorno's writing. In response to "Opera and the Long Playing Record" (Adorno 1990c), Leppert notes that the listener is:

> ... alone and lonely, but his solitude has been turned against loneliness through the trace of intersubjectivity inscribed on the record's grooves. (2002)

Leppert's 'trace of intersubjectivity' is the resonance in recorded music of the immediate and direct interaction that occurs between musician and audience in live performance. This is the basis of Adorno's concept of 'being with', as discussed below.

Adorno discusses the 'antinomy' (1973:18) of modern music, thus capturing the contradiction between the apparently solitary nature of the experience of listening to recorded music on the one hand, and the listener's perception that they experience a kind of interaction with performers on the other. Prior to a full examination of this phenomenon and of being with, it is necessary to examine the consequences of Adorno's understanding that recorded music is a form of communication. Adorno writes:

> Similar to the fate that Proust ascribed to paintings in museums, these recordings awaken to a second life in the wondrous dialogue with the lonely and perceptive listeners ... (1990c:65–66)

To Adorno, music's 'death' is its removal from the singular time and place of live performance by recording. In this death, however, music is resurrected to a new or second life. In Adorno's terms, music's first life is its original playing for the purpose of recording, whether at a live performance or in a recording studio. Once recorded, the original performance is captured and made available for repeated listening; this is the music's second life. Recording thus severs music from the singularity of live performance and releases it for individual listeners who can now spontaneously listen wherever and whenever they choose. Music is no longer tied to the concert hall or to singular performances. In music's second life, lonely and perceptive listeners enjoy recorded music as they would a conversation or dialogue with a friend. Adorno's use of the word 'dialogue' to describe the listener's relationship with recorded music is noteworthy. It captures the sense in which listeners understand their experience of recorded music as a conversation with the musicians concerned.

In another relevant source, Berland also uses telling language. She discusses recorded music in terms of the '... movement of electronically reproduced messages across space ...' (1998:133). Messages are meaningful communications transmitted by a sender to a receiver and, in subsequent discussion, Berland discusses the meanings of messages contained in recorded music. She suggests that '... we find social meanings in the sounds [of recorded music] themselves' (1998:133). Company is one example of a social meaning contained in the sounds of recorded music. It is now appropriate to examine some of Adorno's writings that provide further insight into the nature of this phenomenon.

In a list of variations of what he terms 'entertainment listeners' (1976:16), Adorno refers to the listener '... who kills time and paralyzes loneliness by filling his ears with the illusion of "being with" no matter what ...' (1976:16). Using the term 'being with', Adorno proposes that listeners associate the sound of recorded music with the presence of the musicians who created it, and thus feel accompanied as they listen, even though no musicians are present. This idea forms the basis of company. In Adorno's words:

> The fact that music as a whole, and polyphony in particular—the necessary medium of modern music—have their source in the collective practices of cult and dance is not to be written off as a mere "point of departure" due to its further progress towards freedom. Rather this historical source remains the unique sensory subjective impulse of music, even if it has long broken with every collective practice. (1973:18)

First, it is noteworthy that Adorno refers to music's '... progress towards freedom' (1973:18). This recapitulates the idea, discussed above, that music assumes a second life after recording; it is 'freed' from singular live performances. Second, and specifically related to company, Adorno discusses the modern practice of musical experience and asserts that its routine has its origins in ancient practices of cult and dance, collaborative enterprises in which many people are involved. Adorno argues that these past collaborative practices resonate with contemporary listeners to the point that, although they are physically alone, listeners associate the sound of recorded music with the presence of the collective who contribute to the ritual of live musical performance. In another source, Adorno expresses this idea very clearly, writing that music's '... sound suggests a voice of the collective that will not quite forsake its compulsory members' (1976:43).

Bull refers to Adorno's concept of 'being with' in several of his Walkman studies. In the first, Bull interprets 'being with' as '... the recreation of direct experience by and through technologically mediated forms of experience' (1999:201). In *Sounding Out the City* (2000), Bull writes further that he understands the term 'being with' '... to refer to a qualitative relationship between the subject and that which is experienced' (2000:28). Richard Leppert, in comments regarding Adorno's essay "The Curves of the Needle", also makes observations which aid understanding of Adorno's ideas. Leppert observes:

> ... the Sony Walkman/Discman paradox, wherein the aesthetic labor of others is privately heard rather than experienced intersubjectively and socially as may occur in musical ritual, whether ecclesiastical or secular. (2002:234)

Leppert's explanation of Adorno's thoughts are noteworthy here for their direct reference to the Walkman. They are also applicable to the iPod and other personal audio devices.

In another reference to music's capacity to assuage loneliness, Adorno suggests that music's '... comfort function, the anonymous solace to the congregation of the lonely, ranks surely not lowest among the functions of music today' (1976:43). Adorno subsequently expands on music's ability to comfort lonely listeners, writing:

> By circling people, by enveloping them—as inherent in the acoustical phenomenon—and turning them as listeners into participants, it [recorded music] contributes ideologically to the integration which modern society never tires of achieving in reality. It leaves no room for conceptual reflection between itself and the subject, and so it creates an illusion of immediacy in the totally mediated world, of proximity between strangers, of warmth for those who come to feel the chill of the unmitigated struggle of all against all. Most important among the functions of consumed music—which keeps evoking memories of a language of immediacy—may be that it eases men's suffering under the universal mediations, as if one were still living face to face in spite of it all. (1976:46)

First, Adorno refers here to recorded music in general; however, his reference to recorded music's 'envelopment' of listeners is unexpectedly relevant to portable music which, by virtue of its inherent headphones and stereo image, is experienced by listeners as surrounding them. Second, Adorno observes that the formal distinction between performers and audience members (such as occurs at concert hall performances of Western art music) is broken down in the experience of recorded music, such that listeners can feel involved in the creation of their music. As noted above, Eisenberg mounts a similar argument, suggesting that listeners use recorded music to create solitary rituals in which they participate in any way they choose. Conducting along with the record and playing air guitar are examples of these, and such behaviour magnifies listeners' sense of participation in their recorded music. In sum, Adorno argues that listeners crave human interaction. The solitary experience of recorded music does not involve 'real' or immediate human interaction, but listeners' 'participation' in recorded music creates the illusion of cooperative effort with the recorded musicians. This illusion eases the essential loneliness of solitary listening.

Tetsuo proposes a variation of the experience of company examined to this point, discussing links between multiple mobile listeners rather than between individual listeners and the musicians who created the music they hear. He writes:

> This device [the Walkman or iPod] is for personal use only, so that the users are isolated from each other even if they listen to the same music source. They are united in the way of marionettes. Walkman users form a collectivity of marionettes, maintaining some kind of individualism of the user. When there is a weak pull in the string, the marionette can, to an extent, enjoy a sense of individualism: electronic individualism. When, though, there is a strong pull, the users will be totally integrated into an electronic collectivity... (1984:18)

Tetsuo is the only writer who discusses such a phenomenon, and his thoughts are included here for the sake of completeness. Tetsuo's reference to "the same music source" makes it clear he is mostly referring to radio, a source of musical experience which is beyond the scope of this study.

Several writers other than Adorno discuss the kind of musical experience he was first to observe, each bringing interesting and slightly different perspectives to the discussion. It is now appropriate to review these sources. Eisenberg contributes to an understanding of company as reminiscent of the presence of musicians. He describes listening to recorded music as:

> ... a séance where we get to choose our ghosts. The voices we hear come from another world—something voices are good at. So there is a certain bafflement: the voice seems to be coming from the medium, or the loudspeaker, but where is it really coming from? Sight, in the habit of tracing the sound to its source, finds nothing but some wooden boxes and a spinning circle. At the end of the search for focus one finds a surd. The performer becomes (in the etymological sense) occult. (1988:57)

Eisenberg's reference to the 'spinning circle' relates to the mechanism of the gramophone, but his ideas can be applied to any means by which recorded music is reproduced. Moreover, by using the term 'occult', which, in the etymological sense, means 'hidden', Eisenberg suggests that the sound of recorded music directly implies the presence of musicians who, because they cannot be seen but only heard, are understood by the listener to be somehow hidden from sight as they play. Further, a 'surd' is a sound uttered with the breath and not the voice. Such a sound, although diminished to an extent, is not disembodied and requires a human speaker to enunciate it. Thus, although it might be considered in some ways diminished in comparison with live music (as a whisper is to the speaking voice), listeners understand the sound of recorded music to convey something of the presence of musicians who created its sounds in the first place. In another reference to the gramophone and to its horn in particular, Eisenberg eloquently describes the crux of music's role in company. He asserts 'You can stare into the horn and know that at some vanishing point beyond the visible concavity there is someone breathing' (1988:64). Eisenberg's reference to outdated technologies of sound reproduction does not invalidate his point. He maintains that listeners associate the sound of recorded music with the human endeavour required to produce it in live performance, even though recorded music is reproduced by inanimate means. Listeners thus have a sense of the presence of musical performers when they hear recorded music.

Cubitt mounts a similar argument regarding sound in general, rather then music. He observes that sound:

> ... was always placed because it was always physical. It burbled up from the wet viscera of the body, the tumbling of water, the impact of bronze on wood, to fill the space of the ear, the valley, the battlefield. (1998:102)

Original sounds have meaning for those who hear them because they are associated with particular events. The tumbling of water is associated with a waterfall; the sound of bronze on wood was associated with battle; the perceptions of eye and ear are linked in original experience. Related to recorded music, Cubitt suggests that the reception of recordings is more complex because they take '... fidelity, rather than construction, the false materialism of the replication of origin' (1998:102) as their goal. That is, listeners understand recordings in terms of the musicians who created them rather than understanding them to possess an aesthetic of their own. It is in their reference to the musicians concerned that, as Cubitt argues:

> ... recorded sounds gain their discretion, their ability to mediate between people over spatio-temporal distances, as relations between people rather than things. (1998:103)

Thus, as listeners associate the sound of tumbling water with a waterfall, they associate the sounds of recorded music with the musicians who would create them in performance rather than with the technology of sound recording and reproduction which actually enables them to hear it.

Bull and Chen, although they do not use the terminology of this study, both observe company in the course of their own studies. Bull, in particular, proposes that 'The personal stereo gives users a sense of companionship. They "know" their music and never feel "alone" whilst listening to it' (2000:189). Bull also discusses users' motivation, writing '... the primary motive is to fend off feelings of isolation through the mediated company of personalized "sounds". Personal stereos provide company' (2000:189). Although he is not explicitly discussing portable music, Bull refers to listeners 'knowing' their music and to listeners' 'personalised sounds' (2000:189). Clearly portable music, not the device that transmits it, is the key to company.

Chen also describes a mode of Walkman use among college students that relates to company. She names this mode 'Emotional Companion' (1993:101) and observes that '... listening to a Walkman provides companionship for many students' (1993:101). It is significant that both scholars observe company in the course of their studies, even if they mistake the Walkman rather than portable music as the source of the companionable feelings that listeners experience.

In response to the advent of recorded music and the Walkman, both Theodore Gracyk and Crispin Sartwell call for a new understanding of what constitutes social interaction. While discussing the social aspects of the experience of recorded music, Gracyk reviews other writers' criticisms which, while allowing that '... recorded music affords acquaintance with musical works ...' (1997:143), maintain this acquaintance is debased. Such objections are based on the belief that '... musical performance is something more than the presentation of sequenced sound' (1997:143). Frank Howes is one who takes this view. He discusses a perceived inadequacy of recorded music related to its nondependence on musicians or other human input and writes that '... aesthetic boredom always hovers close over either the desiccated or the condensed forms of music, because the human contacts are remote and precarious' (1926:37). Timothy Day further elucidates Howes' position well: 'Musical performance is of its essence communication and requires human presence and the interaction of players with an audience ...' (2000:209). Howes considers recorded music inferior to live music because it lacks the element of human interaction. Gracyk takes a broad view in rebutting this position, observing that:

> ... the success of recorded music means that familiar standards of integrity, developed in conjunction with the music-making technology of the last few hundred years, will be superseded by new standards. (1997:144)

Gracyk thus maintains that old assumptions, appropriate when music was only ever a live experience, are not relevant to recorded music. The impression of the presence of musicians is the basis of company. Some might suggest that the presence of musicians is related to live musical experience and company is thus an example of exactly what Gracyk criticises. The presence of musicians is, however, vital to the experience of recorded music. Without musicians to create it in the first place recorded music would not exist and it is the impression of the presence of such recording musicians that mobile listeners enjoy in company.

Finally, Gracyk observes another common complaint concerning recorded music. Whereas, in the live performance situation, audience members 'experience themselves as a community, not as separated individuals' (Thom, cited in Gracyk 1997:147), some writers object to recorded music on the basis that 'Recordings reduce us to mere voyeurs' (1997:147). In response, Gracyk applies the argument reproduced above; that is, recorded music requires a different analytical approach from that needed for live music. He observes many new types of interaction which occur between those who listen to recorded music (examples include Jamaican sound system trucks, the British rave scene and musical discussions on the internet [see Gracyk 1997:147]) and concludes that '... the social formation typical of live performance gives way to a different social formation when audiences favour recorded music over live performances' (1997:147). Company is another example of a new social formation associated with portable music. Rather than the direct and immediate interaction between musicians and audience members that occurs in live performance, mobile listeners have the impression of a form of interaction based around music and with musicians as they listen alone.

Sartwell's argument is similar to Gracyk's. He refers directly to the Walkman rather than to recorded music and heralds the emergence of a new mode of social interaction as a consequence of its development. In the first place, Sartwell observes a general disapproval of mobile listeners '... hiding in their tiny room of sound, disconnected from the people around them' (1999). Sartwell notes 'Many argued that this heralded a dark new era of isolation: It's just you and your machine' (1999), but disagrees with this common reaction, suggesting that Walkmans:

> ... have a social aspect: Even as they separate us from other people, they are also ways we connect to one another. The Walkman is, after all, a vehicle for the mass media, whether you're listening to Dixie Chicks or sports on the radio. (1999)

Sartwell believes this is indicative of a more general trend, manifest in such technologies as the networked laptop computer, the pager and the mobile phone. He writes 'Civic participation is not declining; rather the meaning of both "civic" and "participation" are changing' (1999). Company is clearly a new form of civic participation, facilitated by developments in the recording and reproduction of music yet beholden to musical practice set down before recording was a possibility or even an idea. Before recorded music listeners had to attend concerts or other live musical events in order to interact with performers. Since recorded music, listeners have been able to enjoy this experience at their leisure. The Walkman and iPod facilitate a further leap in convenience such that listeners can assuage their loneliness and enjoy musical communication with their favourite performers in practically any situation.

Chanan also notes conventional concepts of social interaction and observes they become irrelevant in the face of technological development. Chanan first refers to Benjamin to explain how '... the age-old dialogue of musical communication was radically upset' (1995:8) as recordings became a common avenue of musical experience. He then notes:

> Above all, the technique of reproduction—mechanical, electrical or electronic—creates a distance, both physical and psychic, between performer

and audience that simply never existed before, which produces new ways for music to be heard and allows the listener totally new ways of using it. (1995:8)

The understanding that recording distances listeners from performers is conventional. The result of this distancing—the new ways in which Chanan suggests listeners can use recorded music—are the subjects of this study. Further, listeners' impressions that the distance between themselves and performers is somehow bridged as they listen to portable music is the essence of company. Chanan does not examine this bridging any further but Gracyk and Sartwell, reviewed above, aid understanding of the concept.

To return briefly to Adorno, we see that his discussion in "The Curves of the Needle" (1990a) is pertinent to this discussion. He writes:

> The turntable of the talking machines is comparable to the potter's wheel: a tone-mass is formed upon them both, and for each the material is pre-existing. But the finished tone/clay container that is produced in this manner remains empty. It is only filled by the hearer.[1] (1990a:55)

This argument relies on the metaphor of the gramophone's turntable, but is equally applicable to other means by which recorded music is reproduced. Adorno observes that recordings are unable to reproduce anything other than music's sound. Any element of the listener's experience beyond the sound of the music (company is one example of such an element) is brought to the experience by the listener.

Kathleen Higgins contributes to examination of the nature of the interaction that portable music facilitates between listeners and performers. Although she does not use this study's terminology, Higgins clearly expresses the essence of company. She writes:

> Music is, by its very nature, a social activity. Even the music heard through the earphones of a Walkman sounds like it comes from an external reality. In fact it does come from outside the individual listener. A social relationship between those who produce it and the listener still occurs, albeit a highly mediated one. But in addition, I believe that most listeners experience music, even that which comes to them through earphones, as a kind of communication between themselves and other human beings. (1991:151)

Higgins suggests that the sound of portable music comes from an external reality. This is aligned with Adorno's concept of 'being with',

•CHAPTER FOUR•

in which recorded music carries connotations of live musical practice. Aligned also with Sartwell's understanding that portable music is mass media that 'connects' listeners to others, Higgins suggests listeners understand that music, even recorded music such as portable music, is a form of communication. This communication is sufficient to forge a social relationship, distant though it might be, between performer and listener. Musical communication as the basis of listeners' perceptions of interaction with musicians is an idea Adorno also expresses, as noted. Higgins, however, differs fundamentally from Adorno when she suggests recorded music facilitates an actual 'social relationship' between performers and their listeners. Adorno asserts no such relationship is possible and any interaction listeners perceive between themselves and performers is a figment of their imagination.

The difference between Higgins' and Adorno's positions is a matter of perception. On the one hand, Higgins is content, first, that recorded music is a means of communication and, second, that listening and responding to such musical communication represents a form of actual interaction. On the other hand, although he acknowledges that music is a form of communication, Adorno feels that solitary listeners cannot simply wish social interaction into being as they listen to recorded music. He does not set out his minimum requirements of 'real' social interaction but implies a form of dialogue is necessary, rather than the distant monologue that recorded music represents. For individual listeners also, the experience of portable music is a matter of perception. If a listener perceives an interaction with the musicians concerned as they listen, then that is sufficient for them and should be sufficient for scholars studying their experience. This experience is not diminished if another listener does not experience their portable music in that way, even if the second listener dismisses the possibility of such interaction.

Now, having reviewed sources that discuss so many different perspectives on the idea of company, including the need for new definitions of 'social' and 'interaction' and of 'civic' and 'participation', the foolishness of evaluating recorded music by the standards of live music, and ideas related to music as communication, it is appropriate and timely to turn to this study's interviews for real listeners' understandings of this experience.

Campbell recognised that his portable music facilitates a kind of relationship between himself and the performers on the recordings. He recounted:

> Because there's not a lyrical content to most of the music I listen to there's not the lingual or poetic "I understand what you're saying" kind of thing but there is a kind of connection in a sort of non-personalised way. I'm not thinking about them [the musicians concerned] as individuals or persons. They're more like other beings who are really enjoying the shape and structure of the sound. I share a common enjoyment in the structures that they present. (2001)

It is noteworthy that Campbell listens to music without lyrical content, testimony to music's capacities as a medium of communication even in the absence of words. Campbell enjoys the '... shape and structure of the sound' (2001) and feels the performers concerned would have a similar enjoyment of these aspects of their own work. Thus, Campbell feels he has something in common with the performers and this is the basis of the connection he feels with them as he listens.

John listens to portable music while running for exercise. Asked why, John responded:

> I basically use it to keep me company. I never have the Walkman on when I run with someone else so it's basically just for company. (2001)

John clearly enjoys listening to portable music while running because the music eliminates any feelings of loneliness and makes his exercise more pleasurable. This exemplifies company as a function of portable music, exploited by mobile listeners to modify and improve lonely aspects of their daily lives.

Function Eight: Aural Mnemonic

In aural mnemonic, listeners use portable music to prompt memories of past events. In the classic example of this function, a person hears certain music during a memorable moment in her/his life (this initial hearing need not involve a Walkman or iPod; live music or recorded music in any form can be effective). The music then becomes associated with the person's memories of that moment and she/he is reminded of it when they subsequently re-hear it on their Walkman or iPod. In this way, the person's thoughts, emotions and feelings are not directed toward their surroundings or their immediate situations or even toward their portable music as they listen, but toward memories of their past.

Adorno addresses issues relevant to aural mnemonic in two sources. First, in *Introduction to the Sociology of Music* (1976), he writes that 'Music is nonobjective and not unequivocally identifiable with any moments of the outside world' (1976:44). This is an important qualification. Music is never directly or immediately associated with nonmusical objects or phenomena and it is only in listeners' thoughts that such links are drawn. A listener's understanding of an association between an event and music merely reflects the random concurrence of the music with an event in the listener's history in the first place, then subsequently with the listener's memory of that event. Second, in "The Form of the Phonograph Record" (1990b), Adorno understands recordings are '... the first means of musical presentation that can be possessed ...' (1990b:58). Then, specifically relevant to aural mnemonic, Adorno draws a comparison, observing that '... records are possessed like photographs ...' (1990b:58). Adorno's comparison between recorded music and photographs illustrates the link between recorded music and listeners' memories of past events. Even for people who do not feature in the image or who did not take the picture, photographs can prompt memories of the past; they are visual mnemonics. Musical sounds are sometimes contrived to resemble sounds associated with nonmusical objects or events in a manner which could be compared to a photograph's iconic representation of a scene. Apart from this relatively crude association, music is never explicitly and indisputably associated with extramusical concepts or objects in the way a photograph is an image of other things. Nevertheless, music can prompt memories in those who experience it in the manner a photograph can for people who view it and this is the basis of aural mnemonic.

Adorno subsequently uses another metaphor in discussing the association between recorded music and listeners' lives. He writes that phonograph record albums are:

> ... herbaria of artificial life that are present in the smallest space and ready to conjure up every recollection that would otherwise be mercilessly shredded between the haste and humdrum of private life. (1990b:58)

Once again, Adorno's reference to phonograph records is relevant to the discussion of other formats of recorded music. A herbarium is a space that houses a collection of dried plants and Adorno's metaphor is apt. He suggests that, in the music captured within them, recordings preserve listeners' memories, thus helping listeners recreate the emotions and feelings associated with the events of their lives. Adorno implies a degree of desperation on the listener's part, as if the busyness and mundanity of their existence threaten the imminent destruction of their memories. In this light, recorded music's mnemonic role is all the more remarkable, filling the listener's need for a personal narrative as respite from the toil and monotony of their lives.

The perfect repetition inherent to recorded music has already been observed to play a role in listeners' experiences of portable music's functions, especially environmental control and company. David Hamilton also discusses such repetition, noting that:

> ... for some listeners (and perhaps occasionally for all of us), the unchanging aspect of recordings can be pleasing and reassuring; they can act as aural security blankets, particularly if they have extra-musical associations. (1980:69)

Hamilton's observations regarding recordings' '... extra-musical associations ...' (1980:69) clearly relate to aural mnemonic. However, Hamilton's observations suggest other motivations in listeners' use of portable music; namely, listeners gain enjoyment and comfort from listening to portable music which reminds them of aspects of their pasts and this comfort, in addition to the memories themselves, motivates their nostalgic listening.

In what amounts to a general background of aural mnemonic, DeNora writes:

> At the most general and most basic level, music is a medium that can be and often is simply paired or associated with aspects of past experience. It was part of the past and so becomes an emblem of a larger interactional, emotional complex. A good deal of music's affective powers come from its co-presence with other things—people, events, scenes. In some cases, music's semiotic power—here, it's emblematic capacity—comes from its conditional presence; it was simply "there at the time". In such cases, music's specific meanings and its link to circumstances simply emerge from its association with the context in which it is heard. In such cases, the link, or articulation, that is made—and which is so often biographically indelible—is initially arbitrary but is rendered symbolic (and hence evocatory [sic]) from

its relation to the wider retinue of the experience, to the moment in question. (2000:66)

First, DeNora mentions that music's affective powers for listeners can relate to its co-presence with other people. Relevant to aural mnemonic's social aspects, this passage illustrates the caveat outlined above; although no immediate social interaction takes place, music can prompt listeners' memories involving other people and the emotions associated with those relationships. To that extent, similar to the listening experience in company, discussed above, the experience of aural mnemonic can be social. Second, DeNora's account is of particular interest because it delves more deeply than other sources into the bases of music's associations with other events of listeners' lives. She confirms the general understanding of aural mnemonic, observing that music achieves this association through simple 'pairing' with other events; it was there when the event occurred. DeNora, however, makes an important point, commenting that this linking is entirely arbitrary since particular music becomes associated with particular events purely by chance, possibly resulting in obscure combinations. Third, DeNora observes that links between music and listeners' memories are often indelible. Although she provides no empirical evidence to support this observation and it is difficult to imagine a study that could confirm it, it is sobering that certain music could prompt memories for the rest of listeners' lives. Depending on listeners' feelings toward their memories, music's persistence could necessitate lifelong strategies of avoidance. Finally, DeNora makes reference to '... music's specific meanings ...' (2000:66), suggesting they '... simply emerge from its [music's] association with the context in which it is heard' (2000:66). As the basis of aural mnemonic, it is interesting that DeNora refers to such associations as music's 'meaning'. Meyer is a notable writer who is aware that listeners can perceive music's meaning in a number of ways, including '... exclusively within the context of the work itself [or] in the perception of the relationships set forth within the musical work of art' (1956:1). This does not negate DeNora's claim that listeners perceive personal meaning in music's associations with extramusical objects or events, as Meyer also acknowledges. However, it is important to recognise this is not the only means by which listeners perceive meaning in their music. Aural mnemonic is the outcome of only one of a number of ways in which music can have significance for listeners.

Like DeNora, Kenney refers to recorded music's capacity to become associated with listeners' memories of people. In writing his book he had access to '... 2644 returns from an alleged 20 000 surveys Edison, Inc. claimed to have sent out' (1999:205) '... asking Americans in 43 states to list their "favourite tunes"' (1999:5). Some precursors to aural mnemonic can be observed in the responses that Kenney documents. For example, he reports:

> Many customers recalled and reaffirmed familial love and family identity by replaying recordings of music that they felt pointed to particular departed family members. Respondents preferred "old music well rendered", music that "takes us back to Grandfather days", tunes that brought "memories of home", old tunes that "take us back to the days of childhood". A striking number of Edison's customers wrote that the emotions stirred by their favourite records brought back treasured memories of their grandparents, parents, husbands, wives, and departed sisters, brothers, and children. (1999:8)

Kenney's research presents examples of vivid associations in listeners' minds between their music and their personal lives. The significance of these associations for listeners comes through in this extract, even as they are filtered through Kenney's analysis and writing. Discussion of 'treasured memories' and references to 'departed family members' indicate the potential for great intensity in the experience of recorded music. They also demonstrate music's capacities to generate new modes of social interaction, even for solitary listeners. In a manner similar to that discussed relative to company, recorded music may evoke listeners' memories of relatives and friends as well as the emotions associated with those memories.

A review of certain facets of music psychology provides insight into listeners' experiences of aural mnemonic. Sloboda discusses relevant aspects of the field including affect, music's capacity to influence listeners' feelings and emotions. Regarding affect, he states that 'It is one of the most inescapable and characteristic features of music that people report strong emotional reactions to it' (2001:544). Sloboda subsequently analyses affect in terms of two processes. The first of these is extrinsic affect. The second is intrinsic affect, in which listeners understand music to express emotion either iconically, through some resemblance between the music and the event, or symbolically, where the listener's response is determined by an appreciation of ' ... formal and syntactic properties of the musical sequence' (2001:545). Intrinsic affect is discussed in detail below as it informs the examination of mood management. Regarding extrinsic affect, Sloboda writes:

> Certain types of stimulus (including music, smells and tastes) seem to become associated in human memory with particular contexts or events in earlier life, and provide a trigger to the recall of these events. (2001:545)

Sloboda notes that this takes place particularly when the original events were '... occasions of strong emotion' (2001:545). To Sloboda, the emotions related to past events of listeners' lives are fundamental to extrinsic affect. He notes that specific pieces of music can trigger strong emotions which lead listeners' '... attention away from the present music on to the remembered past event' (2001:545). In another study, Sloboda examined listeners' chosen personal uses of music. Related to aural mnemonic, he found 'The use of music as a cue to reminiscence is the single most frequent use reported' (1999:360). In line with Sloboda's analysis, in aural mnemonic, portable music may be seen to first trigger listeners' emotions and, second, trigger listeners' memories of events during which they experienced those emotions. Sloboda's thoughts are significant here because they bring discussion of listeners' emotions to the fore. This concept has been hinted at to this point, but not explicitly addressed; as cited above, DeNora observes music's evocative powers and Kenney refers to recorded music's capacity to bring about emotions associated with listeners' memories of deceased relatives. Bull and Gumpert both describe Walkman use that relates to the individual experience of aural mnemonic and, like Sloboda, expand discussion of aural mnemonic from memories to also include emotions, feelings, and fantasies. First, Bull suggests that listeners:

> ... become absorbed with the flow of their memory sparked off by the sounds emanating from their personal stereo. They don't look [at their surroundings], rather they recreate the feelings and sensations of whatever their memory conjures up before them. (2000:188)

Corresponding with Sloboda's thoughts, cited above, Bull observes that, in addition to listeners' memories, portable music also prompts feelings and sensations. Bull also emphasises listeners' 'removal', in a manner similar to that discussed pertinent to boundary demarcation, from their surroundings. Second, Gumpert discusses the runner, listening to portable music, who:

> ... is distracted from the pain of running or avoids the monotony of the daily route. In such situations the original sound source is separated from its new use and environment. Energy is directed inward, the visual images induced by the sound not congruent with the task at hand. The music triggers memories and fantasies, while muscle and motor coordination operate in the routine world. (1987:90)

Gumpert notes a sharp distinction between a listener's 'routine world' and the memories and fantasies that portable music triggers for her or him. In the runner's case, this distinction facilitates more enjoyable exercise. Use of portable music in aural mnemonic is not, however, restricted to fitness devotees but prompts reminiscence and removes listeners' attention from their surroundings in many different situations. As implied by both Bull and Gumpert, mobile listeners might use portable music intentionally to evoke pleasant memories of their pasts. This is another instance of mobile listening in which the 'side effects' of listening, rather than portable music itself, is the focus of listeners' attention. Conversely, it is also possible that a mobile listener, not anticipating the potency of their particular music, could accidentally trigger memories and emotions. This leads to the possibility that mobile listeners could unsuspectingly subject themselves to unpleasant memories and emotions, which, although undesirable, would nonetheless be an example of aural mnemonic.

On turning to this study's interviews, the first impression is the relative fewness (2 of 26) of respondents whose listening corresponds to aural mnemonic. This is a far smaller return than the 50 percent of respondents documented in Sloboda's research. This study's more specific focus on portable music might explain the discrepancy: Sloboda drew no distinction in the type of listening he examined. The generally older demographic Sloboda surveyed might also be a factor since 30 of Sloboda's 45 female respondents and 28 of his 31 males were older than 40 years, a total of 58 respondents from 76. By contrast, only 3 of this study's 26 respondents were older than 40 years. It is possible, had the respondents been directly questioned about aural mnemonic, that a greater proportion would have related relevant experiences. Nonetheless, the accounts reproduced below are excellent illustrations of the individual experience of aural mnemonic. First, Daniel recounts:

> Even now the music that I was listening to at that time [during high school] has a really big effect on me. Things like the second Powderfinger album, although I'm a little ashamed to admit that now, and this band called

Smudge, their album *You Me Carpark ... Now*. If I hear that music now I'm transported back to that time and place.[2][3] (2001)

When he re-hears the music he was listening to at that time, Daniel is strongly affected by emotions and memories corresponding to his time at high school. Daniel is not entirely consumed by his memories while listening. He is aware of his own response and thus recounts his embarrassment at what he now considers a lapse in his musical taste.

Second, Shoji described portable music to which he will no longer listen because of the memories it prompts. He recalled:

> ... I have a whole heap of CDs that I used to listen to when I was studying in Year 12 but I don't like listening to them any more. It just reminds me of that. (2001)

Like Daniel, Shoji associates particular music with his high school experiences. For Shoji this is not a particularly pleasant reminiscence and is reason enough for him to avoid listening to those recordings. Shoji's account of his listening demonstrates how aural mnemonic does not always involve pleasant memories.

Function Nine: Mood Management

Mobile listeners use portable music to achieve or preserve a desired mood, for example, to help get them started in the morning, maintain their productivity at work, overcome irritability, annoyance or even aggression, and relax in order to get to sleep at night. One of the earliest references to interplay between music and listeners' moods is found in Aristotle's *The Politics* (1992 [c330BC]). Aristotle writes:

> Now in rhythm and in tunes there is the closest resemblance to the real natures of anger and gentleness, also of courage and self-control, and of the opposites of these, indeed of all the other kinds of character; and the fact that hearing such sounds does indeed cause changes in our souls is an indication of this. (1992 [c330BC]:465)

Aristotle observes a resemblance between human character and the sounds of music. His concepts of 'character' and 'soul', which exist in states such as courage and self-control, are broader than the contemporary concept of mood, which is a state of mind or feeling. In contemporary terms, courage and self-control are thought to be personality traits rather than moods. However, Aristotle's 'character' can also exist in a state of anger. Anger is understood today as a mood, suggesting a contemporary understanding of mood is an element of what Aristotle discusses as character. Aristotle's *The Politics* exemplifies one difficulty which arises when reviewing most sources which pertain to mood management. Aristotle discusses music's effects on the character and on the soul. Other writers discuss music's effects on listener's emotions and feelings. Despite these variations in terminology, each of the sources reviewed here informs this examination of music's effects on mood. Pertinent to the examination of mood management and in contemporary terminology, Aristotle understands that music can prompt a shift in the listener's mood and suggests music's influence on mood is a result of resemblance between them.

In his review of affect, discussed below, Sloboda dismisses the nature of the relationship between music and listeners' moods which Aristotle proposes. Sloboda writes it is a feature of the relationships between music and emotion:

> ... that a listener can recognise or identify the emotion represented without actually feeling it. A necessary consequence of iconic recognition is a cognition such as "this is happy music". This may lead to a further cognition, "this music makes me feel happy", but there is no necessity for this further step. (2001:545)

While Aristotle's understanding of the nature of the interplay between music and listeners' moods is questionable in the light of modern psychological understanding, his writing is noteworthy in that it demonstrates the lengthy history of the idea. Music has long been understood to influence listeners' moods and mood management is a single recent instance of this broader phenomenon.

The seventeenth and eighteenth centuries saw a noteworthy development in the understanding of the interplay between mood and music. Mentioned briefly above, the concept of the 'affects' developed from the principles of rhetoric. According to the European musical aesthetic prevalent during this time, the affects were '... rationalized emotional states or passions ...' (Buelow 2001:181) which the composer should move in listeners as a good speaker would move the emotions of her or his audience. Composers setting texts to music, '... sought to express in their vocal music such affects as were related to the texts ...' (Buelow 2001:181) and thus unify the various elements of their work. Mattheson, one of the more significant Baroque writers on this topic, gives over substantial portions of his treatise, *Der Vollkommene Capellmeister* (1981 [1739]), to categorising types of affect as well as the affective connotations of various musical components. He writes that music's influence on the affects is the most important and significant of all music's qualities. Other baroque writers also dedicated parts of their treatises to discussions of the affects, including Mersenne (see 1957 [1636-7]), Kircher (see 1970 [1650]), Printz (see 1969 [1696]) and Marpurg (see 1977 [1750-1790]). While the explicit, formalised correlations that these writers discussed between specific musical features and listeners' moods are no longer the sole basis of musical practice, a more general connection between music and the moods remained during subsequent musical eras and persists today. This is the basis of mood management, a function of portable music with its origins in the earliest musical philosophy, in musical practice of the seventeenth and eighteenth centuries and, more recently, with its basis in common perception.

Other writers have published their views on the interplay between music and listeners' moods relatively recently. Adorno sets out a typology of music listeners, classified according to the degree of their understanding of the form and structure of the musical work. One classification is the emotional listener, for whom:

> ... the relation [to music] becomes crucial for triggering instinctual stirrings otherwise tamed or repressed by norms of civilisation. Often music becomes a source of irrationality, whereby a man inexorably harnessed to the bustle of rationalistic self-preservation will be enabled to keep having feelings at all. (1976:8)

Here Adorno proposes that music can be a refuge for listeners otherwise consumed by mundanity, providing emotional stimulation and respite in the face of the need to earn a living. Adorno's observation raises the possibility that mood management might be of great importance for some listeners, a matter of necessity. Beyond managing listeners' feelings and moods, in Adorno's somewhat grim vision, music supplies listeners with feelings they otherwise could not experience.

DeNora conducts a study in which she examines the ways individuals use music in their daily lives. One conclusion is that '... music is an active ingredient in the organization of self, the shifting of mood ...' (2000:61). Of particular interest is DeNora's allusion to the means by which music influences people's moods, or the ways people relate to music that enable it to act in this way. DeNora is certain that music's intrinsic qualities alone cannot change a listener's mood. Rather, she believes that listeners interpret music in such a way that it holds certain emotional significance for them. Music only influences listeners' moods as a result of this extrinsic emotional significance. DeNora does not investigate this phenomenon further, but music's particular qualities, which give it emotional significance for listeners and the capacity to influence their moods, are examined fruitfully by music psychologists.

Sloboda, one such music psychologist, examines music's relationship with listeners' moods, offering many useful insights. As noted in the examination of aural mnemonic, and similar to DeNora's ideas, cited above, Sloboda draws a distinction between 'extrinsic' and 'intrinsic' affect. In extrinsic affect (see 2001:545) music becomes associated in human memory with contexts or events in earlier life and triggers recall of those events when it is subsequently heard. This is called extrinsic affect because music's significance is derived from its association with nonmusical, external events. Then, relevant to mood management, Sloboda also discusses intrinsic affect (2001:545-546) in which music itself is related to emotional responses in two ways. First, in the iconic relationship, there is '... some formal resemblance between a musical structure and some event or agent carrying emotional "tone"' (2001:545). Sloboda gives the example of loud, fast music, which '... shares features with events of high energy and so suggests a high-energy emotion such as excitement' (2001:545). Second, the symbolic relationship comes about '... where the listener's response is determined by an appreciation of formal and syntactic properties of the musical sequence' (2001:545). Sloboda (1992) examines these properties of music in detail in and suggests that music can prompt emotional responses in listeners and thus influence their moods by either means, or by a combination of both.

Of great interest, Sloboda also discusses the general features of music which enable it to elicit strong emotions to a greater extent than other art forms, observing three key characteristics. First:

> Music unfolds over time and so is capable of engaging the emotions of expectation and expectations realized or dashed more effectively than static forms ... (2001:544)

Second, '... music uses directly, and often mimics, the most emotionally important signal of the human species: the voice ...' (2001:544). Third:

... music engages the auditory sense, which gives it a general arousing capacity due to the fact that we cannot escape the source of stimulation ... as well as providing a link to the most primitive and fundamental feelings and experiences of human life. Infants have an inter-uterine auditory life of some complexity well before they are able to engage the other senses to the same degree. (2001:544–545)

The combination of these factors gives music a powerful capacity to influence listeners' moods.

Discussed above relating to aural mnemonic, Kenney examined the results of a survey Edison Inc. carried out in 1921 to determine the musical preferences of its customers. Kenney's study demonstrates that music's capacity to influence listeners' moods is not only employed by listeners to influence themselves; people sometimes play recorded music in attempts to influence the moods of others. Among the survey returns he examines, Kenney recounts:

> Many female respondents revealed that they strengthened family ties in those tired irritable hours late in the afternoon when relations become brittle. One mother got her children to dance to "The Home Dances". Another revealed that: "We have all moods of music. Some one looks *blue* or a little peeved [and] I go in and start "Henry Jones Your Honeymoon is Over" and at once everybody smiles and the white flag waves". (1999:10–11, italics in original)

Kenney demonstrates that people have used recorded music from the early days of its availability in attempts to influence others' moods. Party hosts, would-be seducers and film makers are a few examples of people who might use recorded music to influence other's moods and manipulate emotional responses, illustrating the common understanding that music has an effect on listeners' moods.

Bull, Chen, and Moebius and Michel-Annen all describe Walkman use that informs the examination of mood management. First, Bull writes that walkman 'Use ... helps them [listeners] to change their mood in the desired direction' (2000:189). Second, Chen writes 'The purpose of using a Walkman is to facilitate the individual experiencing certain mood' (1993:97). Finally, Moebius and Michel-Annen (1994) write:

> ... they [Walkman listeners] can select the sounds which are best suited to their mood. Thus they can either intensify the feeling they have, or change it. (1994:573)

These sources all make the same point; that is, mobile listeners feel portable music influences their mood and take advantage of its convenience to manage their moods as they feel the need. This assertion is supported by interview results. For example, and with an evocative turn of phrase, Nigel stated:

> Good walkman music can make you a superhero when just walking down the mall. A nice triumphant rock song can have you feeling like a million bucks walking down the street. (2001)

Carl has an interesting perspective on his portable music. Discussing the effects of listening to portable music on other, concurrent, activities, he explained:

> It makes some things more relaxing. I find that if I start listening to a familiar tune it sort of gives me a lift inside and I want to do more things. I might be down and out and then I hear a piece that I taped a few years ago and I think "Oh yeah, that's really good". It gives you that sort of feeling that you're driving in a car and you go through a speed camera and you know you're over the speed limit and you don't get a ticket. (2001)

While the pleasure Carl expresses at hearing some portable music might reflect his approach to driving more than his approach to music, it is nonetheless apparent that his portable music can change his mood. It relaxes him and gives him 'a lift'.

Shoji is another mobile listener who takes advantage of portable music's capacity to influence his mood. He stated:

> It does change your mood a bit. If I'm annoyed I put on some thrashy music to make me feel better. (2001)

The main point to come out of Shoji's listening is the causal relationship he draws between given music on the one hand and mood outcomes on the other. This demonstrates the awareness some people have of their moods and of the effect music has on them, even to the extent they can 'self-prescribe' music to correct undesirable moods.

Darryl's listening is noteworthy for the dramatic effect of his portable music on negative moods. Discussing how he chooses what to listen to, Darryl reflected:

> It can all depend on what sort of week I'm having at work, or things might be going on at home, I don't know. The music reflects the way I feel at times. I love my music so it can probably reflect how I'm feeling. If I've had a bad day at work I want some real heavy stuff, I think, just to get rid of my anger

rather than going out and smashing something, kicking the cat. I reckon it's a really great release for me. (2001)

Portable music is clearly a means by which Darryl, like Shoji, modifies negative feelings. Darryl's account of his listening recalls Rösing's (see 1984:123) suggestion that music can temper aggression. Whether Darryl would actually smash something without the release provided by his portable music is unknown. Nonetheless, it is clear Darryl values his chosen heavy music because it helps him to vent feelings of anger and frustration without resorting to antisocial behaviour.

Campbell is also aware of portable music's mood-altering properties. Asked when he listens to portable music, he responded:

> I use it [portable music] to change my mood. I put on music specifically when I'm going for a walk to pump me up or mellow me out. (2001)

In the first place, Campbell's mood is improved as a result of listening to portable music. This subsequently optimises his walking, either for exercise or reflection. This is the first example identified during interviews of a listener using portable music to achieve more than one resulting mood, to 'pump me up' or mellow me out'. Campbell's account illustrates portable music's broad capacities relative to listeners' moods and thus in mood management.

Like Campbell, Fiona recounts that she listens to portable music at work because she knows it can influence her mood in several ways. She related:

> I like to keep a selection of my own CDs at work. I find that different styles of music are appropriate at different times depending on my mood, stress level and type of work. If I have had a stressful day then I generally prefer to listen to music that is easy listening and calming. This helps to alleviate tension and get the creative juices flowing. When designing I often need to block out distractions and I use music to do this. I know that certain CDs will put me in different moods. Some of my music leaves me feeling positive and enthusiastic. Other music helps me to mellow. Other music makes me want to dance on my desk and sing at the top of my lungs, which is probably not recommended in my office! (2001)

Fiona uses portable music in a way which demonstrates several of its functions. She listens to block out distractions in the manner of environmental control, while simultaneously choosing music to achieve various moods as they are appropriate for different working situations. This illustrates the potential for overlap between portable music's various functions, with mobile listeners achieving several simultaneous outcomes by listening. Also, relevant to mood management alone, Fiona's listening is another example of portable music's capacity to influence listeners' moods in several directions and thus illustrates its utility as a means of mood management.

Function Ten: Time Management

In time management, mobile listeners feel that listening to portable music is a more worthwhile pursuit than other activities in which they could engage. Accordingly, people listen to portable music instead of resigning themselves to doing nothing or instead of undertaking activities they consider boring or monotonous. Mobile listeners thus claim time they might otherwise have considered wasted for a purpose they consider of value and thus manage their time to best effect. Time management is a simple function to understand. It relies on mobile listeners' perceptions of their own listening in comparison with other things they could be doing. If they consider listening to portable music to be more worthwhile and consequently listen rather than doing something else, then their listening can be described in terms of time management.

Adorno presents ideas pertaining to time management, although, he rejects the possibility that listening to music can be a fulfilling use of time which listeners might otherwise consider wasted. In a general observation of music's role for some listeners, Adorno writes that music can be '... the decoration of empty time' (1976:47) and that it '... "beats time", copying the chronometric beat, and in doing so "kills time" ...' (1976:49). Recall the discussion, presented in Chapter Three, of listeners' personal sense of time as a means of boundary demarcation. That examination of musical time and its relation to chronometric time relates to Adorno's comments as they are presented here. Adorno's observations correspond to portable music's role in time management, however his use of the word 'decoration' is noteworthy. Adorno feels music cannot actually hold real significance for listeners when they listen only to pass the time. He suggests that music heard in this way can only distract listeners from the passing of time in which they are otherwise unoccupied. In this instance it is likely Adorno's opinion is the product of a somewhat elitist viewpoint. As noted, Adorno considers only 'expert' (1976:4) listening '... fully adequate ...' (1976:5). Expert listening involves achieving complete understanding of the form and structure of complex musical works at first hearing and is impossible for most listeners. For the great majority, however, as discussed in chosen sounds and as Adorno notes himself (see 1976:14), music is entertainment or an agreeable occupation. The basis of time management is that, rather than resigning themselves to boredom or to monotony, listeners enjoy listening to portable music that entertains and diverts them and this is nothing to be sneered at.

Earlier discussion of aestheticisation, in which it was noted that listeners engaged with their surroundings and thus demonstrated their place within a collective environment, resonates in the examination of time management. As was the case in aestheticisation, listeners' engagement with their surroundings is taken as evidence that they exist within a collective society which consists as much of its physical manifestations as it does of the people who live within it and construct it. Bull describes mobile listeners' relationships with their environments, writing:

> City life is often experienced as repetitive and users are often consumed with their oppressive routine. They describe taking the same journey to work every weekday, forty-eight weeks of the year. They might also be fed up and bored with their job, their routine and their journey. They know each step of the daily journey with its predictable monotony, every station and how long it will take them to cover their daily journey. They feel oppressed by it. They have long ceased to take any notice of their surroundings. The use of the personal stereo is the only thing that makes the time pass bearably for these users. At least while they listen to it they do not have to think about their daily routine or the office that awaits them. (2000:190)

Bull discusses this strategy of Walkman use in terms of listeners' monotonous working routines with particular reference to commuting on public transport. This reflects the trend of the literature relevant to time management, in which discussion of listeners' use of music to make good use of their time is often couched in terms of travel. Berland's writing is no exception. She narrates an account of driving at high speed along a familiar road while listening to music and observes:

> It doesn't feel like space that interrupts the affinity between me and my destination, but rather time, punctuated by landmarks and musical endings, which together signal the episodic triumph of individual movement over the density of landscape, of time over space. (1998:130)

Berland mentions the landmarks that punctuate her journey. This suggests music cannot entirely remove her attention from the real physical space through which she is traveling. Nonetheless, Berland thinks of the distance she must travel mainly in terms of the time it takes. In turn, she defines her traveling time in terms of the music she plays as she drives. Her trip is defined by the musical endings she hears before arriving at her destination. In this way Berland claims otherwise monotonous travelling time for her own pleasurable musical experience. If Berland were using a Walkman or iPod to listen, this would be a classic instance of time management but, as it stands, her example demonstrates time management's origins in earlier musical practice related to recorded music.

Chambers forwards a similar opinion in an article in which he specifically discusses the Walkman. Chambers refers to the modern or contemporary 'nomad' for whom the Walkman is '... a significant symbolic gadget ...' (1994:51). For these listeners, Chambers asserts:

> ... the older, geometrical model of the city as the organiser of space has increasingly been replaced by chronometry and the organisation of time' (1994:52).

Berland and Chambers observe that, for the traveling listener, whether on a long distance car trip or within a city, music defines travel in terms of time rather than distance. With musical accompaniment, travel becomes a sequence of musical episodes rather than a struggle against physical distance. Thus time spent traveling—time some would resent and consider ill spent in comparison what they anticipate upon their arrival—can be redeemed by music. Mobile listeners are equipped to take advantage of this phenomenon at any opportunity.

This study's interviews revealed several examples of mobile listening practice that throw light on individual mobile listeners' experiences of time management. Firstly, Darryl discussed the motivation for his daily mobile listening while he commutes on trains:

> [When I listen to portable music] I don't have to listen to people talking on the train. I can just zone out. It's just my way of escaping. It saves me communicating with anyone else. That way I can just relax totally because I don't get much chance to relax at home or at work. It's my way of just totally zoning out. (2001)

The interpersonal mediation aspects of Darryl's listening are discussed above. Pertinent to time management, portable music also enables Darryl to completely relax in a manner impossible for him at work or home. In enabling him to zone out in this way, Darryl's portable music allows him to claim his commuting time for something he would otherwise be unable to do. Note that Darryl is not focussed entirely on his portable music, but on the relaxation it provides in the manner of mood management. This suggests a previously undiscussed aspect of time management; that is, listeners consider music's 'side effects', relaxation in this instance and not just the music itself, to be relatively productive occupations. Darryl's listening is another illustration of possible complexities of examining portable music's functions. Here portable music is observed to simultaneously operate in three different functions for one listener, chosen sounds, time management, and mood management.

Nigel's mobile listening also takes place on public transport. He related:

> I went through a phase recently when I found that I had a whole load of tapes that I'd never got around to listening to. Not really having too much in the way of tape players around the house, listening to them on the Walkman on the buses was really handy. (2001)

Portable music's convenience enables Nigel to claim commuting time for his own enjoyment and for activity he considers productive. Further, as noted, portable music's functions often overlap and Nigel's listening can be considered in terms of chosen sounds as well as of time management. Nigel's portable music is obviously material to which he wants to listen.

Scott's listening further illustrates portable music's multiple simultaneous functions. He stated:

> I use it [the Walkman] to listen to music, obviously because I like music, and it helps pass the time on the bus as well. It's better than just sitting on the bus. (2001)

As is the case for most listeners, portable music functions as Scott's chosen sounds; he states '... I like music ...' (2001). Scott's account of his listening clearly marks it as an instance of time management as well; '... it helps pass the time on the bus ...' (2001).

Brugh's listening is also best described in terms of a combination of time management and chosen sounds. Discussing his experiences on public transport, he stated:

> You know there's the saying, 'time flies when you're having fun.' I'm having fun because I'm listening to music, so the trip goes faster. (2001)

The 'fun' Brugh experiences while he listens illustrates that his portable music entertains him and thus functions as his chosen sounds. Brugh exploits this enjoyment to manage the time he spends on public transport and transform an otherwise unpleasant experience. This is time management.

Continuing the theme in which listeners' accounts of time management involve various forms of transport, Katerina related her own mobile listening experience in the back seat of her parents' car:

> Well my parents listen to talkback radio almost all the time. If I listen to music the time just goes by because I enjoy what I am listening to. If I didn't have my Walkman I would be listening to talkback radio, which to me is really boring, and time would seem to drag. It's a bit like the saying "Time flies when you're having fun". Well I consider it fun listening to music I like. (2001)

Interestingly, Katerina considers time spent traveling with her parents to be boring primarily because she has to listen to talkback radio. She reclaims this time for her own enjoyment by listening to portable music. Katerina's interview response indicates that people can consider time wasted for a number of reasons. Portable music's convenience allows many people to convert such situations into opportunities for activity they consider fruitful or enjoyable. Both Brugh and Katerina used the expression 'time flies when you're having fun' to describe their mobile listening. This phrase is a hallmark of time management.

Miriam also referred to public transport. Asked to compare time spent on the bus with and without portable music, she replied:

> It goes a lot more quickly [with portable music] because I've got something to distract me and I've got something to do. So I much prefer travelling on the bus when I've got a Walkman or a Discman. It makes it a whole lot more pleasurable I guess. I feel like I've actually done something by the end of my bus trip rather than just sitting there and doing absolutely nothing. (2001)

Miriam, a music student, enjoys her bus trip when she listens to portable music. Moreover, Miriam considers her mobile listening to be a constructive activity. It gives her the opportunity to achieve something useful during her bus trip and thus take advantage of time that could otherwise be wasted.

Stephen's account of his mobile listening on bus trips is very similar to that of Miriam. He related:

> I guess it [portable music] just keeps your mind occupied. It gives you something to listen to. I suppose the same sort of thing would happen if I were reading a book. It's really just to take up some time by doing something profitable. (2001)

Stephen's observation that portable music enables him to do '... something profitable' (2001) clearly indicates that his listening is an instance of time management. Stephen's portable music enables him to make best use of time that might otherwise pass unprofitably with activity Stephen considers worthwhile.

Function Eleven: Activation

In activation, listeners move to portable music's rhythm and, aware of the stimulation they receive, sometimes take advantage of it in order to exercise or work more productively. An early account of music's capacity to stimulate physical activity in listeners is found in Aristotle's *The Politics* (1992 [c330BC]). Discussing the modes, Aristotle asserts '... the Phrygian puts men into a frenzy of excitement' (1992 [c330BC]:466). Subsequently discussing different types of rhythm, he observes '... some give rise to vulgar movements' (1992 [c330BC]:466). While intriguing, Aristotle's concern with the vulgarity of some movements is unimportant to this discussion. It is noteworthy, however, that he observed the movements to occur and perceived that they were stimulated by music.

Other examples of music's capacity to catalyse movement, more recent than those observed by Aristotle, are present in the literature. Sloboda, for instance, conducts a broad survey of peoples' everyday uses of music. He finds that 22 percent of his respondents use music while running, cycling or driving. The cyclists and runners in this group are probably using portable music in activation. Other listeners within Sloboda's sample use music to accompany their housework (22 percent) and whilst exercising (4 percent). It is impossible to discern the form of recorded music Sloboda's respondents use, although these listeners are probably using it in a manner related to activation. Portable music might be used by some but presumably not by all and, by definition, those instances where portable music is not involved cannot be considered activation. Nonetheless, Sloboda's research demonstrates music's involvement with physical activity for many listeners.

DeNora also observes a number of situations in which music is employed specifically for its capacity to regulate movement. Some of her examples relate to work. They include sea shanties that are used '... for a variety of specialised tasks on board a ship—hauling sails and heaving heavy weights such as the anchor' (2000:105) and waulking songs sung by weavers:

> ... while going through the motions of hand-shrinking the cloth, a process that involves pulling and beating the cloth, moving from one end of the bolt to the other. (2000:104)

DeNora also examines music's role in aerobics exercise sessions. She finds that music is critical in helping instructors to successfully motivate and warm-up members of their classes and then extract maximum physical effort from them (see DeNora 2000:89–102). DeNora's discussion is aligned with Mowitt's. As noted in the introduction, Mowitt (1987:190) discusses as the 'recontextualisation' of musical masterpieces as the soundtrack for health routines. Dance, more often than not performed to musical accompaniment, is another example of the relationship between music and human movement (Julia Sutton *et al.* [2001] explore the nature of this relationship in an excellent article which includes an extensive bibliography to aid further reading). These are all examples of the alignment of bodily movements with musical rhythm, and thus illustrate the common perception that music influences movement. Activation, involving portable music, is only one example of this general phenomenon.

Bull discusses a strategy of Walkman use which, as noted, aids this study's definition of activation. He writes that listeners '... describe feeling energized. The music, with its steady rhythm, helps them in this' (2000:190). Lind similarly observes that 'It [portable music] gets you going, or keeps you going when you need energy' (1989:59). Finally, as noted, Gumpert observes:

> It is ... strange to witness a person gyrating and foot-tapping to an imperceptible beat. The suspicion of a possible mental disturbance vanishes

with the sight of an earphone, and the alien walks and jogs to the beat of a different tape. (1987:91)

Gumpert discusses mobile listeners in this passage and the gyrations he observes are instances of activation. Portable music is ideal in this role. Apart from its musical qualities, rhythm paramount among them, portable music can accompany listeners in most places and as they undertake most forms of activity or exercise. Aquatic activities have been the obvious exception but it seems this obstacle might have been overcome with the development of the 'Swimman' (2003).

Interviews revealed examples of mobile listening that corresponded to activation. Aliese, for example, recounted her experiences of simultaneous mobile listening and walking:

> I think it's a thing that's been conditioned into me from years of aerobics or whatever. I just want to move in time with the music and if people get in my way I can't. You've got to stop but the music just keeps going and you want to try to go along with it. (2001)

The rhythm and tempo of Aliese's portable music influences her walking to the extent that she is annoyed to have to stop while the music continues. Aliese attributes her particular susceptibility to the rhythm of her portable music to her experience with aerobics exercise, but portable music influences the movements of a broader range of people than only aerobics exercisers. For example, Lorrin chooses to listen to portable music while running for exercise. Discussing whether portable music influences the pace and intensity of her exercise, Lorrin recalled:

> It has done. When I first started running with the Walkman I was running to the beat which was a bit of problem because if there was a fast song I was getting tired quickly. (2001)

This is a clear example of activation in which portable music's rhythmic qualities directly influence the listener's physical movement. In Lorrin's case, the rhythm of her portable music was overly effective and pushed her to attempt exercise beyond her capacity.

John also listens while he runs and his experiences are similar to Lorrin's. He stated:

> Sometimes I get conned into a good tune and I try to keep up with the beat, but that's only sometimes. Usually I'm too buggered to keep up with some of those beats. (2001)

Until tiredness becomes a factor, the rhythm of Lorrin's and John's portable music influences the pace at which they exercise. Such examples demonstrate listeners' practical application of portable music's functions to manage aspects of their everyday lives. Lorrin's and John's listening also relates to the functions of music proposed by Merriam, one of which is 'The function of physical response' (1964:223). Merriam asserts '... the fact that music elicits physical response is clearly counted upon in its use in human society ...' (1964:224). Some mobile listeners count on this function in their daily lives and take advantage of portable music's capacities in order to achieve personal goals. In terms of visible outcomes, activation is probably the most obvious demonstration of portable music's functionality for individual listeners.

Notes

[1] Thomas Y. Levin, who translated this essay, includes a footnote at this point. It is reproduced here:

> Adorno plays here upon the untranslatable polyvalence of Ton, which in German means both "sound" or "tone" and also "clay". A Ton-Masse is thus a quantity or mass both of acoustic and of argillaceous material. (1990a:55)

[2] Powderfinger is an Australian rock band.
[3] Smudge is an Australian indie rock band.

• CHAPTER FIVE •

Conclusions

This study has examined mobile listeners and demonstrated ways in which they manage significant portions of their everyday lives through music. Its defining premise has been that the experience of mobile listening is inherently musical; as mobile listeners work or study, traverse urban environments or exercise, their everyday undertakings are transformed by music. Using an analytical approach that accurately reflected mobile listeners' own perceptions of their listening, the study examined a relatively new and, to this point, virtually unexamined genre of musical experience.

The relative infrequency with which listeners concentrate on their portable music was initially surprising; this occurs only in chosen sounds and learning. Moreover, this focussed listening is related to music enjoyment only in chosen sounds. Significantly, in terms of numbers of functions, the majority of listeners would seem to enjoy their portable music principally because it eases their interactions with their surroundings and helps them manage aspects of their lives. This conclusion represents a significant and consequential shift from the common understanding that people mostly listen to music because they enjoy it.

Two comments are necessary regarding methodology. First, the functions of portable music were examined here by extensive review of the literature, in combination with interviews with mobile listeners. This allowed deliberation regarding the extent to which the literature reflected mobile listeners' thoughts about the functions that portable music fulfils for them. It is now evident that, in most cases, the literature represented listeners' experiences accurately. Second, once it was adjusted to recognise music's role in mobile listeners' experiences, Bull's (2000) study provided an excellent methodological foundation. It should be reiterated that the Walkman and the iPod are integral components of portable music, but they are effectively useless without music for them to transmit. It is in the combination of music and its transmission by the Walkman and iPod that portable music gains its distinctive character and the functions examined in this study become possible.

This study's interviews were conducted with respondents exclusively resident in Adelaide, Australia, thus prompting the question: are the results indicative of mobile listening in other locations? Review of published literature based on similar fieldwork in other locations (see especially Bull 2000; Chen 1993; Lind 1989) suggests this study's results are similar to those that have been and potentially would be achieved in other locations.

The interdisciplinary approach of music psychology would seem to hold potential for further understanding music's effects on listeners. Neuroimaging and brain wave research also appear to be powerful tools with great potential for fruitfully examining aural experience. These techniques could generate a useful understanding of music's capacities, especially in relation to listeners' emotions and physiology. Whereas this study notes listeners' use of music according to their intuitive knowledge of its effects on themselves as derived from past experiences and according to anecdotal knowledge, a deeper understanding of music's actions in these situations might lead to useful therapeutic applications.

During this study, and especially in the discussion of interpersonal mediation, it became apparent that mobile listening generated vigorous opinions and responses when it modified listeners' interactions with other people. It is interesting to speculate whether subsequent technological developments, most significantly the mobile telephone, have also received hostile receptions for this reason. Mobile listening initially stood out to observers because it was a form of behaviour, previously considered private, in which people suddenly engaged in public. Moreover, mobile listening engages the ears (unlike using a laptop computer or personal organiser or reading), thus potentially eliminating interactions more emphatically than distractions that engage only the eyes. Mobile telephony is similar to mobile listening in both respects. However, whereas only a relatively undecipherable and small portion of portable music leaks into the public soundscape, people engage in mobile telephone conversations at much higher volumes to the extent that one complete side of the exchange is audible to bystanders. It is possible that mobile listening prepared people for mobile telephony and generally tempered what otherwise could have been problematic bystander reactions.

Examining the history of portable music's functions prompts two questions. First, has music long held these functions or did they only arise with the Walkman's development? Second, did they arise in response to social circumstances, or purely as a result of listeners' whims? Within these concluding remarks it is appropriate to review each function with these questions in mind.

When examining chosen sounds it was noted that people often listen to music because they enjoy it. This is the classic individual experience of portable music. In this case, portable music's portability makes such musical enjoyment possible at every time and in every place listeners desire it. Similarly, regarding learning, it seems probable that would-be musicians have always listened to music to assimilate existing practice. Portable music enables them to listen and study at any time as an individually directed experience. Thus, in the case of both learning and chosen sounds, the Walkman and iPod have simply served to modify and facilitate common and longstanding musical functions which have involved social interaction in the past but which are now individual in nature.

Regarding aestheticisation's first mode, listeners at a live musical event might well perceive the music they hear as aural accompaniment to or augmentation of the visual impression made by their surroundings. This could also occur in response to forms of recorded music other than portable music, and the advent of the video clip has simply given listeners a convenient metaphor with which to describe the experience. Portable music extends this possibility, allowing listeners to accompany mundane images with music and thus transform their everyday individual experiences and social interactions. Regarding aestheticisation's second mode, it was noted that John Cage first prompted the understanding that ambient noise, alone or together with other, planned musical sounds, could comprise aesthetically significant aural experiences. Once again, portable music expands music's preexisting potential. Listeners can now combine sounds from their everyday experience with their chosen music, creating a unique aesthetic and social experience as they do so. Thus, in aestheticisation's first mode, portable music facilitates an expansion of music's long-standing potential. In aestheticisation's second mode, portable music expands musical possibilities that listeners have consciously acknowledged for the last fifty years or so since John Cage made the initial breakthrough. In both modes, the location of individual listening is transformed through the listeners' interactions with their surroundings.

Several examples of the use of recorded music to overcome ambient noise were noted when examining environmental control, but no examples were found of live music being used in this way. Recording allowed listeners to play music at the time and place of their choosing, as the need arose to block out intrusive ambient noises. Environmental control, involving only portable music, subsequently lent listeners the capacity to modify their soundscape wherever they traveled. It appears environmental control is a relatively new function of music, existing in a precursor form only since recording and modified to its final form with the development of the Walkman and subsequently the iPod. Here listening occurs as listeners interact with their environments.

In the examination of boundary demarcation it was noted that animals and insects used sound to demarcate their territory. Although examples of related use of recorded music were observed, there was no evidence of the use of live music in this territorial role. Boundary demarcation would appear to be a recent manifestation of this phenomenon, presignified with recording and, subsequently with the Walkman's development, enabling listeners to demarcate an imagined, yet nonetheless effective, boundary around themselves wherever they are. It is an example of listeners' response to their environments.

Regarding interpersonal mediation, it is significant that, in the initial discussion, there were no examples in which any music other than portable music was observed to modify personal interactions. The earliest relevant example was that of Morita (see 1986:80) testing a prototype Walkman and annoying his wife in the process. Since portable music was involved in this example, the obvious conclusion is that interpersonal mediation is a new function of music, made possible only with the development of the Walkman. However, on reflection a more nuanced situation seems likely. Previously, at a concert of western art music for example, personal interactions would have been more or less suspended for the duration. The concert situation represents what might be called a multilateral modification of personal interactions in which all parties concentrate on the music rather than on social interactions with fellow audience members. By contrast, portable music, heard by a single listener, brings about a unilateral modification. The mobile listener, intentionally or otherwise, modifies interaction between themselves and others. Bystanders are unable to hear the music in question yet have no choice in their modified interactions with the listener. With this in mind, it seems prudent to think of interpersonal mediation as a modification, brought about by the development of the Walkman, of an effect on personal interactions that music has held for some time. Interpersonal mediation is mobile listeners' response to their social environments.

In its initial examination, it was noted that company is a case of portable music recreating the experience of live music in listeners' minds. Listeners associate the sound of their portable music with the presence of the musicians who would create it in live performance, and use it as a substitute companion. In examining the relative novelty or otherwise of company, it is necessary to distinguish between music as a real or literal form of personal interaction, as occurs in live performance, and music as pseudo-interaction, as occurs in company. Clearly, listening to music only becomes a form of pseudo-interaction when music is divorced from the necessary presence of musicians. Music as an antidote to being alone only became possible, and necessary, when musicians were no longer required to create it. By definition, no audience member is alone when musicians are present and playing music for them. Paradoxically, it seems clear that music has functioned in company, or in a manner similar to it, only since it could be heard in the absence of musicians; that is, since it could be recorded and subsequently reproduced. Company then, is a relatively new function of music, forecast with the development of recording and subsequently modified with the Walkman to fulfil listeners' needs to overcome loneliness in any situation. As such, it represents a unique combination of individual and social experience that builds on historical antecedents.

By contrast, the basic concept behind aural mnemonic has existed ever since music held emotional associations for listeners. Portable music only adds the capacity for listeners to experience the memories, emotions, and feelings associated with their music at their convenience. Likewise, the basis of mood management has existed as long as listeners' moods have been influenced by music. Portable music, because of the convenient and mobile listening it enables, allows listeners to manage their moods as they feel the need. Aural mnemonic and mood management are modifications of functions music has historically held since listeners have associated it with their memories or allowed it to influence their moods.

Time management is also a recent modification of a long-standing musical function. Among other motivations, people's choices to listen to music often manifest their belief that listening is a more worthwhile pursuit than other options. Portable music's convenience simply enables people to choose listening on any occasion that it represents a better occupation than other possibilities. Similarly, in the initial discussion of activation, it was noted that music has long influenced listeners' movements. Aristotle (1992 [c330BC]) observed this many millennia ago. The Walkman and iPod, however, give listeners the capacity to listen to music of their choice as they engage in the activity of their choice. Never before have individual listeners been conveniently able to accompany mobile activity such as running or cycling with music. It must be concluded that activation is a recent modification by individual listeners of a fundamental property of music.

The experience of portable music initially appears to be a solitary one. However, scholars as well as the testimonies of several interviewees called into question the true nature of the solipsism that mobile listeners achieve, suggesting that mobile listening is deceptive in its solipsistic appearance. In summary, three indicative scenarios, described here in order from most disconnected to most connected, illustrate listeners' possible involvement with their surroundings. Firstly, a mobile listener who listens to portable music for the sake of the music and gets caught up in the experience might well be as disengaged from their surroundings as appearances suggest. Secondly, listeners' perceptions of their environments might change as they listen so that, in the manner of aestheticisation, listeners enjoy a modified appreciation of their surroundings. Finally, mobile listening might represent the listener's link with certain aspects of their environments even as they attempt, or appear, to cut off contact with them. Paradoxically, listeners' reactive attempts to withdraw from their surroundings might confirm their presence within them. Similar to the manner in which mobile listeners' experiences can combine aspects of several functions, their experiences can also combine elements of the three scenarios described here.

Portable music represents music's democratisation to the level of the individual listener. Prior to recording, some musics, notably western classical music, were not necessarily available to everyone who might have wanted to hear them. Recording was one step in making more music available to more people. The Walkman extended this democratisation still further, making all music equally subject to listeners' choices regarding how it should be used. The iPod, with its associated downloading paradigm of music acquisition, has extended this development yet further again. Portable music is the epitome to date of music's capacity to satisfy individual listeners' needs.

Bibliography

Note: For reasons of privacy, interviews are cited here by first name only. Full documentation is held by the author.

Aaron. 2001. Interview. Adelaide, Australia, October 17.
Adler, Eric. 1999. *Culture Hasn't Been the Same Since Portable Stereo* [electronic newspaper]. reporter-news.com [cited 28 March 2001]. Available from: http://www.reporternews.com/1999/features/culture0920.html.
Adorno, Theodor W. 1967. "Valéry Proust Museum." In *Prisms*. London: Neville Spearman Limited, 173–185.
Adorno, Theodor W. 1973. *Philosophy of Modern Music*. Translated by A. G. Mitchell and W. V. Bloomster. London: Sheed and Ward.
Adorno, Theodor W. 1976. *Introduction to the Sociology of Music*. Translated by E. B. Ashton. New York: Seabury Press. Original publication: 1962.
Adorno, Theodor W. 1978. "On the Fetish-Character in Music and the Regression of Listening." In *The Essential Frankfurt School Reader*, edited by A. Arato and E. Gebhardt. New York: Urizen Books, 270–299. Original publication: 1938.
Adorno, Theodor W. 1990a. "The Curves of the Needle." Translated by T. Y. Levin. *October* 55 (Winter): 49–55. Original publication: 1928.
Adorno, Theodor W. 1990b. "The Form of the Phonograph Record." Translated by T. Y. Levin. *October* 55 (Winter): 56–61. Original publication: 1934.
Adorno, Theodor W. 1990c. "Opera and the Long Playing Record." Translated by T. Y. Levin. *October* 55 (Winter): 62–66. Original publication: 1969.
Aliese. 2001. Interview. Adelaide, Australia, May 31.
Altman, Rick. 1992. "The Material Heterogeneity of Recorded Sound." In *Sound Theory/Sound Practice*, edited by R. Altman. New York: Routledge, 15–31.
Anderson, Benedict. 1991. *Imagined Communities: Reflections on the Origin and Spread of Nationalism*. Revised ed. London: Verso.
Anon. 1989. Walkman. *The New Yorker*, 2 January 1989, 19–20.
Anon. 1999. Walkman hits the 20-year mark. *The Toronto Star*, 18th November, 1.
Aristotle. 1992 (c330BC). *The Politics*. Translated by T. A. Sinclair. Edited by T. J. Saunders. Harmondsworth: Penguin Books.
Augé, Marc. 1995. *Non-Places: Introduction to an Anthropology of Supermodernity*. Translated by J. Howe. London: Verso.
Barbiero, Daniel. 1989. "After the Aging of the New Music." *Telos* (82): 144–150.

Barthes, Roland. 1985. "Listening." In *The Responsibility of Forms: Critical Essays on Music, Art, and Representation*. New York: Hill and Wang, 258–260.

Bartók, Béla. 1976. "Mechanical Music." In *Béla Bartók Essays*, edited by B. Suchoff. London: Faber and Faber, 289–298.

Bendix, Regina. 2000. "The Pleasures of the Ear: Toward an Ethnography of Listening." *Cultural Analysis* 1: 33–50.

Benjamin, Walter. 1968. "The Work of Art in the Age of Mechanical Reproduction." In *Illuminations*, edited by H. Arendt. New York: Harcourt, Brace and World, 219–253. Original publication: 1935.

Berland, Jody. 1998. "Locating Listening: Technological Space, Popular Music, and Canadian Mediations." In *The Place of Music*, edited by A. Leyshon, D. Matless, and G. Revill. New York: Guildford Press, 129–150.

Bettina. 2001. E-mail Interview. Adelaide, Australia, October 10–22.

Bicknell, David, and Robert Philip. 1980. "Gramophone." In *The New Grove Dictionary of Music and Musicians*, edited by S. Sadie. London: Macmillan. Vol. 7, 620–627.

Blacking, John. 1995. "Music, Culture, and Experience." In *Music, Culture, and Experience*, edited by R. Byron. Chicago: University of Chicago Press, 223–242.

Boorstin, Daniel J. 1973. *The Image: A Guide to Pseudo-Events in America*. New York: Atheneum.

Boorstin, Daniel J. 1974. *The Americans: The Democratic Experience*. New York: Vintage Books.

Braidwood, Steve. 1981. "Six Products that Reflect the Age We're In." *Design* (392): 26–27.

Brown, Lee B. 1996. "Musical Works, Improvisation, and the Principle of Continuity." *The Journal of Aesthetics and Art Criticism* 54 (4): 353–369.

Brown, Lee B. 2000a. "Phonography, Repetition and Spontaneity (Sound Recording, Music, Listening, Experience)." *Philosophy and Literature* 24 (1): 111–125.

Brown, Lee B. 2000b. "Phonography, Rock Records, and the Ontology of Recorded Music." *The Journal of Aesthetics and Art Criticism* 58 (4): 361–372.

Brugh. 2001. Telephone Interview. Adelaide, Australia, October 28.

Buelow, George J. 2001. "Theory of the Affects." In *The New Grove Dictionary of Music and Musicians*, edited by S. Sadie. London: Macmillan. Vol. 1, 181.

Bull, Michael. 1999. "The Dialectics of Walking: Walkman Use and the Reconstruction of the Site of Experience." In *Consuming Cultures: Power and Resistance*, edited by J. Hearn and S. Roseneil. London: Macmillan, 199–220.

Bull, Michael. 2000. *Sounding Out the City: Personal Stereos and the Management of Everyday Life*. Oxford: Berg.

Bull, Michael. 2001. "The World According to Sound: Investigating the World of Walkman Users." *New Media and Society* 3 (2): 209–227.

Bull, Michael. 2002. "The Seduction of Sound in Consumer Culture: Investigating Walkman Desires." *Journal of Consumer Culture* 2 (1): 81–101.

Campbell. 2001. Telephone Interview. Adelaide, Australia, August 10.

Carl. 2001. Interview. Adelaide, Australia, October 30.

Chambers, Iain. 1994. *Migrancy, Culture, Identity*. London: Routledge.

Chanan, Michael. 1995. *Repeated Takes: A Short History of Recording and its Effects on Music*. London: Verso.

Chen, Shing-Ling Sarina. 1993. *The Self, the Community, and the Electronic Media*. PhD Thesis, University of Iowa, Iowa.

Chow, Rey. 1999. "Listening Otherwise, Music Miniaturized: A Different Type of Question About Revolution." In *The Cultural Studies Reader*, edited by S. During. London: Routledge, 462–476.

Connor, Steve. 1999. "... or a New Creative Medium?" In *Settling the Score: A Journey Through the Music of the 20th Century*, edited by M. Oliver. London: Faber and Faber, 307–308.

Cooke, Mervyn. 2001. "Film Music." In *The New Grove Dictionary of Music and Musicians*, edited by S. Sadie. London: Macmillan. Vol. 8, 797–810.

Copland, Aaron. 1937. "The World of the Phonograph." *American Scholar* 6: 27–37.

Crawford, Richard. 1980. "Introduction." In *The Phonograph and Our Musical Life: Proceedings of a Centennial Conference 7-10 December 1977 at Brooklyn College of the City University of New York*, edited by H. W. Hitchcock. New York: Institute for Studies in American Music, Department of Music, School of Performing Arts, Brooklyn College of the University of New York, 57–59.

Cubitt, Sean. 1998. *Digital Aesthetics*. London: SAGE Publications.

Daniel. 2001. Interview. Adelaide, Australia, July 5.

Darryl. 2001. Interview. Adelaide, Australia, August 17.

David. 2001. E-mail Interview. Adelaide, Australia, October 3–10.

Davies, Stephen. 2001a. "Anglo-American Philosophy of Music." In *The New Grove Dictionary of Music and Musicians*, edited by S. Sadie. London: Macmillan. Vol. 19, 621–624.

Davies, Stephen. 2001b. *Musical Works and Performances: a Philosophical Exploration*. Oxford: Clarendon Press.

Day, Timothy. 2000. *A Century of Recorded Music: Listening to Musical History*. New Haven: Yale University Press.

DeNora, Tia. 2000. *Music in Everyday Life*. Cambridge: Cambridge University Press.

Dickers, Scott, ed. 1999. *Our Dumb Century*. New York: Three Rivers Press.

du Gay, Paul, et al. 1997. *Doing Cultural Studies: The Story of the Sony Walkman*. London: SAGE Publications.

Eisenberg, Evan. 1988. *The Recording Angel: The Experience of Music from Aristotle to Zappa*. New York: Penguin Books.

Ellen. 2001. Interview. Adelaide, Australia, October 10.

Eno, Brian. 1983a. "Pro Session: The Studio As Compositional Tool-Part I." *Down Beat* 50 (7): 56–57.

Eno, Brian. 1983b. "Pro Session: The Studio As Compositional Tool-Part II." *Down Beat* 50 (8): 50–52.

Erin. 2001. Interview. Adelaide, Australia, November 15.

Fenichell, Stephen. 1983. "Getting Personal." *Penthouse* 14 (6): 138–141, 170.

Fiona. 2001. E-mail Interview. Adelaide, Australia, October 3–16.

Frith, Simon. 1983. *Sound Effects: Youth, Leisure, and the Politics of Rock*. London: Constable.

Gelatt, Roland. 1977. *The Fabulous Phonograph 1877–1977*. 2nd ed. London: Cassell.

Glenyce. 2001. Interview. Adelaide, Australia, October 9.

Goodall, Howard. 2000. *Big Bangs: The Story of Five Discoveries that Changed Musical History*. London: Chatto and Windus.

Gould, Glenn. 1984. "The Prospects of Recording." In *The Glenn Gould Reader*, edited by T. Page. London: Faber and Faber, 331–353.

Gracyk, Theodore. 1997. "Listening to Music: Performances and Recordings." *The Journal of Aesthetics and Art Criticism* 55 (2): 139–150.

Gronow, Pekka. 1983. "The Record Industry: The Growth of a Mass Medium." *Popular Music* 3: 53–75.

Gumpert, Gary. 1987. *Talking Tombstones and Other Tales of the Media Age*. New York: Oxford University Press.

Hamilton, David. 1980. "Some Thoughts on Listening to Records." In *The Phonograph and Our Musical Life: Proceedings of a Centennial Conference 7–10 December 1977 at Brooklyn College of the City University of New York*, edited by H. W. Hitchcock. New York: Institute for Studies in American Music, Department of Music, School of Performing Arts, Brooklyn College of the University of New York, 65–71.

Hardman, Chris. 1983. "Walkmanology." *Drama Review* 27 (4): 43–46.

Harvith, John, and Susan Edwards Harvith. 1987. "Introduction." In *Edison, Musicians, and the Phonograph*, edited by J. Harvith and S. E. Harvith. New York: Greenwood Press, 1–23.

Headlam, Bruce. 1999. Walkman Sounded Bell for Cyberspace. *The New York Times*, 29th July, 7.

Higgins, Kathleen Marie. 1991. *The Music of Our Lives*. Philadelphia: Temple University Press.

Hitchcock, H. Wiley. 1980. "Response to *Address* by John Cage." In *The Phonograph and Our Musical Life: Proceedings of a Centennial Conference 7-10 December 1977 at Brooklyn College of the City University of New York*, edited by H. W. Hitchcock. New York: Institute for Studies in American Music, Department of Music, School of Performing Arts, Brooklyn College of the University of New York, 1–6.

Hosokawa, Shuhei. 1984. "The Walkman Effect." *Popular Music* 4: 165–180.

Howes, Frank. 1926. *The Borderland of Music and Psychology*. London: J. Curwen and Sons.

Jessica. 2001. Interview. Adelaide, Australia, August 23.

John. 2001. Telephone Interview. Adelaide, Australia, October 3.

Joshua. 2001. Telephone Interview. Adelaide, Australia, November 5.

Katerina. 2001. E-mail Interview. Adelaide, Australia, September 16–October 3.

Katz, Mark. 1999. *The Phonograph Effect: The Influence of Recording on Listener, Performer, Composer, 1900–1940*. PhD Thesis, University of Michigan, Michigan.

Kenney, William Howland. 1999. *Recorded Music in American Life: The Phonograph and Popular Memory, 1890–1945*. New York: Oxford University Press.

Kircher, Athanasius. 1970. *Musurgia Universalis, Sive Ars Magna Consoni et Dissoni (1650)*. (Reprint) Hildesheim, New York: G. Olms.

Kolodin, Irving. 1957. "Who Called that Recording a Performance?" *Theatre Arts* 41: 88–89, 100.

Leppert, Richard. 2002. "Commentary." In *Theodor W. Adorno: Essays on Music*, edited by R. Leppert. Berkeley: University of California Press, 213–250.

Lind, Rebecca Ann. 1989. *You Can Take It With You: Uses and Gratifications of the Personal Stereo*. MA Thesis, University of Minnesota, Minnesota.

London, Justin. 2001. "Time." In *The New Grove Dictionary of Music and Musicians*, edited by S. Sadie. London: Macmillan. Vol. 25, 479.

Lorrin. 2001. Interview. Adelaide, Australia, October 7.

Lysloff, René T. A., and Leslie C. Gay Jr. 2003. "Introduction: Ethnomusicology in the Twenty-first Century." In *Music and Technoculture*, edited by R. T. A. Lysloff and L. C. Gay Jr. Middletown, Connecticut: Wesleyan University Press, 1–22.

Marpurg, Friedrich Wilhelm. 1977. *Eight Works (1750–1790)*. (Microform Reprint) New York: University Music Editions.

Mattheson, Johann. 1981. *Der Vollkommene Capellmeister (1739): A Revised Translation with Critical Commentary*. Translated by E. C. Harriss. Ann Arbor, Michigan: UMI Research Press.

Merriam, Alan P. 1964. *The Anthropology of Music*. Evanston, Ill: Northwestern University Press.

Mersenne, Marin. 1957. *Harmonie Universelle (1636–7): The Books on Instruments*. Translated by R. E. Chapman. The Hague: Martinus Nijhoff.

Meyer, Leonard B. 1956. *Emotion and Meaning in Music*. Chicago: University of Chicago Press.

Miriam. 2001. Interview. Adelaide, Australia, October 9.

Moebius, Horst, and Barbara Michel-Annen. 1994. "Colouring the Grey Everyday: the Psychology of the Walkman." *Free Associations* 4, 4 (32): 570–576.

Morita, Akio, et al. 1986. *Made in Japan: Akio Morita and Sony*. New York: E. P. Dutton.

Morris, Jan. 1989. *Pleasures of a Tangled Life*. London: Barrie and Jenkins.

Mowitt, John. 1987. "The Sound of Music in the Era of its Electronic Reproducibility." In *Music and Society: the Politics of Composition, Performance and Reception*, edited by R. Leppert and S. McClary. Cambridge: Cambridge University Press, 173–197.

Mussulman, Joseph Agee. 1974. *The Uses of Music: An Introduction to Music in Contemporary American Life*. Englewood Cliffs, New Jersey: Prentice-Hall.

Narmour, Eugene. 1990. *The Analysis and Cognition of Basic Melodic Structures: The Implication-Realization Model*. Chicago: University of Chicago Press.

Nathan, John. 1999. *Sony: The Private Life*. Boston: Houghton Mifflin Company.

Negus, Keith. 1992. *Producing Pop: Culture and Conflict in the Popular Music Industry*. London: Hodder and Stoughton.

Newell, Martin. 1999. The Age of the Walkman Lyric Sheets. *The Independent*, 10th August, 15.

Nicholls, David, ed. 2002. *The Cambridge Companion to John Cage*. Cambridge: Cambridge University Press.

Nigel. 2001. E-mail Interview. Adelaide, Australia, September 17–October 6.

Paddison, Max Halle. 2001. "Adorno, Theodor." In *The New Grove Dictionary of Music and Musicians*, edited by S. Sadie. London: Macmillan. Vol. 1, 165–167.

Philip, Robert. 1992. *Early Recordings and Musical Style: Changing Tastes in Instrumental Performance, 1900–1950*. Cambridge: Cambridge University Press.

Printz, Wolfgang Caspar. 1969. *Phrynis Mitilenaeus (1696)*. (Microfilm Reproduction) New Haven, Connecticut: Research Publications.

Rice, Timothy. 1987. "Toward the Remodeling of Ethnomusicology." *Ethnomusicology* 31 (3): 469–488.

Rösing, Helmut. 1984. "Listening Behaviour and Musical Preference in the Age of 'Transmitted Music'." *Popular Music* 4: 119–149.

Sartwell, Crispin. 1999. *Happy 20th, Anti-Social Walkman* [electronic newspaper]. Lexington Herald-Leader [cited 28 March 2001]. Available from:

http://www.kentuckyconnect.com/heraldleader/news/100399/commentarydocs/1003walkman.htm.

Schafer, R. Murray. 1977. *The Tuning of the World*. New York: Alfred A. Knopf.

Schiffer, Michael Brian. 1991. *The Portable Radio in American Life*. Tucson: The University of Arizona Press.

Schönhammer, Rainer. 1989. "The Walkman and the Primary World of the Senses." *Phenomenology and Pedagogy* 7: 127–144.

Scott. 2001. Interview. Adelaide, Australia, October 25.

Sessions, Roger. 1970. *Questions About Music*. Cambridge, Massachusetts: Harvard University Press.

Sessions, Roger. 1971. *The Musical Experience of Composer, Performer, Listener*. Princeton: Princeton University Press.

Shoji. 2001. Telephone Interview. Adelaide, Australia, October 22.

Shorter, D. E. L., and John Borwick. 1980. "Sound Recording, Transmission and Reproduction." In *The New Grove Dictionary of Music and Musicians*, edited by S. Sadie. London: Macmillan. Vol. 17, 567–590.

Sloboda, John A. 1992. "Empirical Studies of Emotional Response to Music." In *Cognitive Bases of Musical Communication*, edited by M. R. Jones and S. Holleran. Washington: American Psychological Association, 33–46.

Sloboda, John A. 1999. "Everyday Uses of Music Listening: A Preliminary Study." In *Music, Mind, and Science*, edited by S. W. Yi. Seoul: Seoul National University Press, 354–369.

Sloboda, John A. 2001. "Affect." In *The New Grove Dictionary of Music and Musicians*, edited by S. Sadie. London: Macmillan. Vol. 20, 544–546.

Smith, Giles. 1995. *Lost in Music: a Pop Odyssey*. London: Picador.

Sony. 1999. *Sony Celebrates Walkman 20th Anniversary* [press release]. Sony Corporation Japan [cited 28 March 2001]. Available from wysiwyg://39/http://www/sony.co.jp/en/SonyInfo/News/Press/199907/99-059/.

Sousa, John Philip. 1906. "The Menace of Mechanical Music." *Appleton's Magazine*: 278–284.

Sparshott, F. E. 1980. "Aesthetics of Music." In *The New Grove Dictionary of Music and Musicians*, edited by S. Sadie. London: Macmillan. Vol. 1, 120–134.

Stephen. 2001. Interview. Adelaide, Australia, October 31.

Sterne, Jonathan. 1997. "Sounds Like the Mall of America: Programmed Music and the Architectonics of Commercial Space." *Ethnomusicology* 41 (1): 22–50.

Steven. 2001. Email Interview. Adelaide, Australia, September 17–October 2.

Stravinsky, Igor. 1962. *An Autobiography*. New York: W. W. Norton.

Sutton, Julia, et al. 2001. "Dance." In *The New Grove Dictionary of Music and Musicians*, edited by S. Sadie. London: Macmillan. Vol. 6, 879–908.

Swimman, Inc. 2003. *Waterproof Music Systems for all Environments* [Website] [cited 27th October 2003]. Available from http://www.swimman.net/pages/859128/index.htm.

Tetsuo, Kogawa. 1984. "Beyond Electronic Individualism". *Canadian Journal of Political and Social Theory* 8 (3):15–20.

Tetsuo, Kogawa. 1988. "New Trends in Japanese Popular Culture". In *The Japanese Trajectory: Modernization and Beyond*, edited by G. McCormack and Y. Sugimoto. Cambridge: Cambridge University Press, 54–66.

Thomas, Brian. 1999. *Walkman Turns 20 And Nobody Cares* [electronic newspaper]. Tired News [cited 28 March]. Available from http://tirednews.virtualave.net/technology/7/story_t7141.html.

Toop, David. 2001. "Environmental Music." In *The New Grove Dictionary of Music and Musicians*, edited by S. Sadie. London: Macmillan, 260–261.

Valéry, Paul. 1964 (1928). "The Conquest of Ubiquity." In *The Collected Works of Paul Valéry: Aesthetics*, edited by J. Mathews. London: Routledge and Kegan Paul. Vol. 13, 225–228.

Vaughan Williams, Ralph. 1963. *National Music and Other Essays*. London: Oxford University Press.

Walter, Bruno. 1964. "Some Thoughts About the Musical Record." *The American Record Guide* 30 (5): 374–375.

Wile, Raymond R. 1977. "The Wonder of the Age (The Invention of the Phonograph)." In *Phonographs and Gramophones: Proceedings of the Edison Phonograph Centenary Symposium 2 July 1977 at the Royal Scottish Museum, Edinburgh*, edited by A. G. Thomson. Edinburgh: Royal Scottish Museum, 9–48.

Will, Patrick T. 1986. "Recording." In *The New Harvard Dictionary of Music*, edited by D. M. Randel. Cambridge, Massachussets: The Belknap Press of Harvard University Press, 684–686.

Williams, Christina. 2001. "Does it Really Matter? Young People and Popular Music." *Popular Music* 20 (2): 223–242.

Williamson, Judith. 1988. *Consuming Passions: The Dynamics of Popular Culture.* London: Marion Boyars.

Wilson, Edward O. 1957. *Sociobiology: The New Synthesis.* Cambridge, Massachusetts: Belknap Press.

Index

Aaron, 18, 29, 40, 70
Adler, Eric, 50, 51
Adorno, Theodor, 15, 16, 22, 23, 32, 35, 61, 62, 66, 67, 73, 74, 75, 76, 77, 82, 83, 85, 86, 93, 98, 99, 107
aerobics, 104, 105
aesthetic, 9, 14, 21, 22, 23, 26, 32, 36, 41, 49, 76, 79, 80, 92, 110
Affect, 86, 87, 88, 89, 91, 92, 93, 94
Aliese, 12, 13, 14, 17, 25, 27, 67, 68, 69, 105
anecdote, 56, 59
antisocial, 67, 68, 97
Apple Computer, 1
Aristotle, 9, 10, 91, 92, 103, 113
aura, 32

Bach, Johann Sebastian, 14
Barbiero, Daniel, 22, 23
Bartók, Béla, 13, 14, 30
being with, 74, 75, 76, 82
Bendix, Regina, 36, 37
Benjamin, Walter, 32, 81
Berland, Jody, 31, 45, 46, 74, 75, 99, 100
book, 1, 2, 18, 54, 55, 67, 88, 103
Boorstin, Daniel, 30

boredom, 80, 99
bourgeois, 15, 16, 62
Brown, Lee, 31
Brugh, 102
Buelow, George J., 92
Bull, Michael, 3, 4, 8, 10, 12, 21, 22, 23, 25, 26, 36, 37, 53, 54, 65, 66, 75, 76, 79, 89, 90, 95, 99, 104, 108, 109

Cage, John, 26, 41, 110
Campbell, 57, 70, 84, 97
Carl, 96
CD, 16, 26, 29, 33, 39, 40, 41, 91, 97
Chambers, Iain, 34, 35, 36, 37, 38, 50, 51, 53, 59, 60, 100
Chanan, Michael, 43, 81, 82
Chen, Shing-Ling Sarina, 21, 54, 55, 65, 66, 79, 95, 109
choice, 8, 26, 52, 112, 113, 114
Chow, Rey, 34, 35, 36, 37, 54
clay, 82, 107
collective, 27, 36, 75, 99
comfort, 38, 66, 76, 86
communication, 35, 38, 57, 60, 63, 66, 67, 74, 75, 80, 81, 82, 83, 84
community, 80
companion, 1, 6, 58, 73, 79, 112

concert, 14, 47, 48, 74, 76, 81, 111
Connor, Steve, 26, 27
content, 3, 4, 34, 41, 61, 64, 83, 84
control, 1, 5, 28, 29, 30, 31, 32, 36, 37, 38, 40, 41, 46, 55, 66, 91
courtesy, 60, 67
Cubitt, Sean, 29, 30, 31, 32, 78, 79

dance, 40, 75, 95, 97, 104
Daniel, 10, 11, 58, 68, 69, 90, 91
Darryl, 43, 44, 55, 57, 58, 60, 70, 96, 97, 100, 101
Davies, Stephen, 9, 46, 47, 48
Day, Timothy, 80
decoration, 98
democracy, 113, 114
DeNora, Tia, 2, 86, 87, 88, 89, 93, 94, 104
deviant, 63
dialogue, 35, 74, 81, 83
discourse, 2, 30, 40, 52
Discman, 28, 72, 76, 102
duet, 15

earphones, 3, 5, 29, 33, 42, 43, 44, 58, 59, 63, 69, 70, 82
Edison, Thomas, 2, 88, 95
Edmunds, Dave, 60
Eisenberg, Evan, 22, 23, 28, 29, 46, 48, 49, 50, 76, 77, 78
elocution, 2
Ellen, 44, 52, 55
emotion, 6, 54, 55, 79, 84, 86, 87, 88, 89, 90, 91, 92, 93, 94, 95, 109, 112

Eno, Brian, 47
entertainment, 9, 75, 99
environment, 1, 4, 5, 10, 17, 20, 21, 23, 24, 26, 27, 28, 29, 30, 31, 32, 34, 35, 36, 37, 38, 39, 40, 41, 42, 43, 44, 46, 49, 52, 54, 55, 59, 60, 62, 63, 64, 65, 90, 99, 108, 111, 112, 113
Erin, 11
everyday, 15, 21, 38, 103, 106, 108, 110
exercise, 1, 40, 84, 90, 97, 103, 104, 105, 106, 108
expert, 98, 99
exposure, 11, 22, 26, 47

family, 2, 6, 15, 16, 88, 95
Fenichell, Stephen, 60
fieldwork, 40, 47, 57, 59, 65, 67, 109
film, 1, 4, 20, 21, 22, 24, 25, 54, 66, 95
Fiona, 39, 40, 97, 98
Freud, 55

Glenyce, 12
Gracyk, Theodore, 79, 80, 81, 82
Gronow, Pekka, 3
Gumpert, Gary, 42, 43, 44, 50, 58, 59, 89, 90, 104, 105

Hamilton, David, 86
headphones, 1, 3, 5, 12, 25, 30, 38, 39, 40, 43, 45, 48, 51, 52, 56, 57, 58, 60, 61, 62, 67, 68, 70, 76
herbarium, 86
Higgins, Kathleen, 82, 83

INDEX

Hosokawa, 33, 34, 35, 36, 37, 40, 60, 61, 62
Howes, Frank, 79, 80

Ibuka, Masaru, 72
interaction, 1, 2, 4, 5, 20, 23, 24, 27, 32, 33, 34, 35, 37, 38, 42, 48, 50, 51, 55, 56, 57, 58, 59, 60, 61, 62, 63, 64, 65, 66, 67, 68, 69, 70, 71, 73, 74, 77, 79, 80, 81, 82, 83, 86, 87, 88, 108, 109, 110, 111, 112
interview, 4, 6, 7, 9, 10, 12, 17, 18, 25, 26, 27, 28, 29, 31, 33, 37, 39, 40, 43, 44, 46, 47, 52, 53, 56, 57, 58, 59, 60, 67, 68, 83, 90, 96, 97, 100, 102, 105, 108, 109, 113
iPod, 1, 2, 3, 4, 5, 6, 8, 14, 15, 16, 22, 23, 24, 45, 56, 57, 59, 61, 62, 64, 66, 76, 77, 81, 84, 100, 108, 110, 111, 113, 114
isolation, 35, 42, 50, 52, 54, 64, 79, 81

John, 13, 14, 26, 41, 84, 105, 106, 110
Joshua, 53

Katerina, 102
Kenney, William, 88, 89, 95
Kircher, Athanasius, 93

leakage, 5, 51, 52, 53, 56, 60, 61
Leppert, Richard, 73, 74, 76
Levin, Thomas Y., 107
Lind, Rebecca Ann, 3, 4, 10, 12, 37, 54, 57, 62, 63, 64, 65, 66, 104, 109

literature, 1, 6, 7, 16, 28, 37, 39, 40, 41, 42, 57, 61, 64, 67, 99, 103, 108, 109
live music, 13, 14, 15, 22, 30, 31, 32, 45, 46, 75, 78, 80, 81, 83, 84, 110, 111, 112
loneliness, 73, 74, 75, 76, 77, 81, 84, 112
Lorrin, 29, 30, 31, 39, 40, 47, 48, 105, 106
LP, 22

Marpurg, Friedrich Wilhelm, 93
Mattheson, Johann, 92
mechanical reproduction, 32
medium, 3, 17, 31, 75, 77, 84, 86
memory, 85, 89, 94
Merriam, Alan, 9, 10, 106
Mersenne, Marin, 93
methodology, 108
Meyer, Leonard B., 87
minidisc, 16, 18, 40, 41
Miriam, 17, 18, 28, 29, 40, 102, 103
Moebius and Michel-Annen, 21, 38, 39, 95
monotonous, 6, 73, 98, 99, 100
mood, 1, 6, 73, 89, 91, 92, 93, 94, 95, 96, 97, 98, 101, 112, 113
Morita, Akio, 56, 57, 59, 69, 72, 111
Morris, Jan, 23
motivation, 1, 10, 11, 14, 37, 40, 42, 66, 68, 79, 86, 100, 113
Mowitt, John, 104
Mozart, Wolfgang Amadeus, 23

music student, 4, 11, 12, 13, 14, 103

Negus, Keith, 50, 51
newspaper, 54, 72
Nigel, 96, 101

Onion, The, 64, 72

pedagogy, 14
performance, 12, 13, 14, 16, 17, 18, 26, 30, 31, 32, 37, 73, 74, 75, 76, 78, 79, 80, 81, 112
personal interaction, 1, 5, 20, 33, 56, 57, 61, 63, 64, 65, 66, 67, 70, 71, 111, 112
personal stereo, 10, 21, 37, 50, 54, 57, 60, 62, 63, 64, 66, 79, 89, 99
philosophy, 93
Philosophy of Modern Music, 73
phonograph, 2, 32, 49, 85, 86
photograph, 22, 85
place, 17, 26, 27, 28, 29, 32, 33, 37, 38, 40, 44, 45, 49, 50, 51, 52, 54, 55, 58, 59, 64, 67, 70, 73, 74, 78, 80, 81, 85, 87, 89, 91, 97, 99, 101, 105, 110, 111
Placebo, 68, 72
Powderfinger, 90, 107
Printz, Wolfgang Caspar, 93
private, 2, 15, 24, 51, 53, 54, 55, 61, 62, 63, 65, 76, 85, 109
productive, 1, 6, 11, 18, 29, 30, 40, 101, 103
Proust, Marcel, 74
psychology, 88, 109
public, 27, 37, 42, 49, 51, 52, 53, 54, 62, 66, 109

public transport, 5, 11, 40, 41, 60, 70, 99, 101, 102

radio, 13, 34, 42, 49, 77, 81, 102
reading, 17, 29, 54, 55, 103, 104, 109
recontextualisation, 104
recorded music, 2, 3, 4, 12, 13, 14, 15, 16, 17, 22, 23, 28, 29, 30, 31, 32, 34, 42, 45, 46, 47, 73, 74, 75, 76, 77, 78, 79, 80, 81, 82, 83, 84, 85, 86, 88, 89, 95, 100, 104, 110, 111
reminisce, 36, 41, 46, 49, 77, 89, 90, 91
repetition, 29, 30, 31, 32, 86
replacement, 28, 38, 40
rhythm, 1, 6, 54, 73, 91, 103, 104, 105, 106
ritual, 17, 42, 75, 76, 77
Rösing, Helmut, 97

Sartwell, Crispin, 79, 81, 82, 83
Schönhammer, Rainer, 62, 63
Scott, 12, 13, 18, 44, 45, 55, 69, 101
sea shanty, 104
second life, 74, 75
secret, 60, 61
Sessions, Roger, 30, 31, 32
Shoji, 46, 47, 91, 96, 97
slide, 3, 8, 22
Sloboda, John, 88, 89, 90, 92, 94, 103, 104
Smith, Giles, 24, 25
Smudge, 91, 107

social, 5, 9, 20, 23, 24, 27, 33, 34, 35, 36, 37, 48, 50, 52, 55, 56, 57, 58, 59, 60, 64, 65, 66, 67, 68, 75, 76, 79, 80, 81, 82, 83, 87, 88, 97, 110, 111, 112
solipsism, 1, 20, 24, 34, 50, 113
solitary, 2, 24, 27, 34, 36, 50, 53, 73, 74, 77, 83, 88, 113
solitude, 20, 74
Sony, 64, 72, 76
soundscape, 5, 28, 29, 34, 35, 37, 38, 40, 63, 109, 111
soundtrack, 1, 20, 22, 23, 28, 104
Sousa, John Philip, 13, 14, 16
Sparshott, F. E., 9
Spice Girls, The, 27
Stephen, 59, 103
stereo image, 43, 76
Steven, 40, 41, 69, 70
Stravinsky, Igor, 14, 15
student, 4, 6, 10, 11, 12, 13, 14, 15, 17, 65, 79, 103
surroundings, 1, 4, 5, 11, 20, 21, 22, 23, 27, 35, 36, 37, 38, 41, 42, 44, 45, 46, 47, 48, 50, 51, 52, 54, 55, 56, 59, 60, 63, 65, 85, 89, 90, 99, 108, 110, 111, 113
Swimman, 105

telephone, 6, 10, 109
television, 49
Tetsuo, Kogawa, 36, 77

theoretical, 1, 4, 11, 13, 15, 26

time, 1, 3, 11, 13, 16, 17, 18, 22, 23, 24, 25, 28, 29, 30, 31, 32, 33, 40, 41, 44, 47, 48, 49, 50, 52, 66, 68, 69, 70, 73, 74, 75, 86, 90, 91, 92, 94, 96, 97, 98, 99, 100, 101, 102, 103, 105, 110, 111, 112
transmission, 12, 31, 37, 108
transmit, 3, 4, 10, 12, 33, 34, 36, 44, 45, 51, 75, 79, 108
transparency, 22
turntable, 22, 82
typology, 4, 93

Valéry, Paul, 48
Vaughan Williams, 15
video, 20, 25, 110

Walkman, 1, 2, 3, 4, 5, 6, 8, 10, 11, 12, 14, 15, 16, 17, 18, 21, 22, 23, 24, 25, 26, 27, 28, 29, 33, 34, 35, 36, 37, 38, 40, 41, 42, 43, 44, 45, 50, 51, 52, 53, 54, 55, 56, 57, 58, 59, 60, 61, 62, 64, 65, 66, 67, 68, 69, 72, 75, 76, 77, 79, 81, 82, 84, 89, 95, 96, 99, 100, 101, 102, 104, 105, 108, 110, 111, 112, 113, 114
waulking, 104
Williamson, Judith, 37, 40, 51, 52, 53

MUSIC
[MEANINGS]

GENERAL EDITORS: STEVE JONES, JOLI JENSEN,
ANAHID KASSABIAN & WILL STRAW

Popular music plays a prominent role in the cultural transformations that are constantly reshaping our world. More and more, music is at the center of contemporary debates about globalization, electronic commerce, space and locality, style and identity, subculture and community, and other key issues within cultural and media studies.

Music[Meanings] offers book-length studies examining the impact of popular music on individuals, cultures and societies. The series addresses popular music as a form of communication and culture from an interdisciplinary perspective, and targets readers from across the humanities and social sciences.

Recent titles include:

    Holly Kruse
    Site and Sound: Understanding Independent Music Scenes

    Janne Mäkelä
    John Lennon Imagined: Cultural History of a Rock Star

To order other books in this series, please contact our Customer Service Department:
    (800) 770-LANG (within the U.S.)
    (212) 647-7706 (outside the U.S.)
    (212) 647-7707 FAX

Or browse by series: WWW.PETERLANG.COM